SUCCESS WITH
ALKALINE-LOVING
PLANTS

SUCCESS WITH
ALKALINE-LOVING PLANTS

Graham Clarke

GUILD OF
MASTER CRAFTSMAN
PUBLICATIONS

First published 2008 by
Guild of Master Craftsman Publications Ltd
Castle Place, 166 High Street
Lewes, East Sussex BN7 1XU

All of the pictures were taken by the author, except for
those listed below:
GMC/Eric Sawford: front cover, back cover (top and fourth down);
pages 1, 2, 8, 18, 19, 74 (right), 79–80, 85, 86 (left), 88 (right),
89–101, 103, 104–106, 107 (left), 108–112, 113 (left), 114–115,
116 (left), 118, 119, 124–128, 130 (bottom), 131, 132 (left), 133,
134 (left), 135–136, 138 (left), 139 (left), 140, 141 (left), 144 (right);
Chris Gloag: 13; Hozelock: 53 (bottom), 75 (left); morguefile.com: 71;
Royal Society for the Protection of Birds: 65; Mr Fothergill's Seeds: 40,
87 (right); Plant World Seeds: 117, back cover (third down);
Priory Farm Garden Centre, England: 72 (right).

ISBN: 978-1-86108-489-7

A catalogue record for this book is available from the British Library.

Associate Publisher: Jonathan Bailey
Production Manager: Jim Bulley
Managing Editor: Gerrie Purcell
Project Editor: Gill Parris
Managing Art Editor: Gilda Pacitti
Designer: James Hollywell
Set in Futura

Colour origination by GMC Reprographics
Printed and bound in Singapore by Kyodo Printing

Contents

CHAPTER 1

What is an 'alkaline' soil?

Although a straightforward question, the answer to it is, unfortunately, rather complex. It is true that an alkaline soil is a chalky soil, but a more precise definition is that it is any soil having a pH level greater than 7.0 (see panel on page 16). Even more fundamental is that an alkaline soil generally sits atop limestone or chalk bedrock.

LIMESTONE AND CHALK LANDSCAPES

The term 'limestone' technically embraces chalk, and chalk white cliffs topped by the greenest of grasses are some of the most welcoming of views to visitors and those returning from trips overseas. Old, rocky limestone lands contrast with these undulating chalk downlands, yet geologically and chemically they are similar.

These landscapes were laid down in tropical seas and lakes as long ago as 200 million years; they comprise the residue of countless billions of nano-planktons (blue-green algae) which, with other creatures, sank to the seabed. A microscopic image of chalk will show a mass of minuscule snails and sea anemones that, over the millennia, have become compressed into rock.

Chemically, these rocks are referred to as calcium carbonate. Weathering of rock tends to be by wind or the action of water, but the latter makes the most dramatic changes in the land's make-up. Acid rain particularly affects chalk and limestone: carbon dioxide from the air dissolves in rain and forms carbonic acid, which can dissolve calcium carbonate. It percolates through natural cracks and fissures in chalk and limestone rock and, over the millennia, these cracks become enlarged, and eventually pieces of rock may become separated from the rest.

Some of the most dramatic landscapes are achieved through the natural convergence of time, weather and chalk or limestone rock.

Undulating chalk downlands (below) are geologically – and chemically – similar to old, rocky, craggy limestone lands (facing page), yet they look totally different.

ABOVE The main nutrients found in soils are nitrogen for leaf growth, phosphorus for root development and potassium for flowering and fruiting. Typical soils will also contain amounts of boron, zinc and copper.

BELOW Areas of clay soil can be prone to flooding.

SOIL MAKE-UP

Typical alkaline soils over chalk and limestone bedrock are an oatmeal colour, and they drain rapidly after rain. They are generally stoney, but light and comparatively easy to dig.

It may be that your alkaline soil is also a clay soil. This will be noticeable in that it bakes hard, and cracks when dry, and is practically impossible to dig in a dry summer. Conversely, in winter after rains, snows, frosts and thaws, it is a sticky, gloopy mess. The area may also be prone to flooding after heavy rains. Some gardeners like to add gravel to such soils, in the belief that it opens the soil and improves drainage. This may be correct if the soil is only slightly clay. However, in heavy clay the addition of gravel makes the overall soil more concrete-like in summer. I find it is better to add coarse fibrous farmyard manure, or masses of bulky garden compost. If this is added annually over a number of years, there will be a marked improvement in the structure and integrity of the soil. Such improved soils can grow the most beautiful of plants, that are frequently unsuccessful in drier conditions.

THE 'GOODNESS' IN ALKALINE SOILS

The main nutrients a plant needs are nitrogen for leaf growth, phosphorus for root growth and potassium for flowering and fruiting. These key nutrients are widely spread in most soils, but in alkaline soils the phosphorus becomes unavailable to acid-loving plants (known as calcifuges) such as camellias, rhododendrons and heathers.

Also, many plants find it more difficult to access the minor (but nevertheless essential) nutrients, the more alkaline the soil becomes. These nutrients include the so-called 'trace' elements of iron and manganese (involved in the manufacture of chlorophyll), as well as boron, zinc, copper and molybdenum.

Symptoms of plants that are growing in a soil that is too alkaline for them include:

- A general yellowing
- Veining and scorching of leaves
- Small new leaves
- Premature death of foliage and small branches.

Such symptoms indicate that the plant is 'chlorotic', and gardeners often refer to this as 'lime-induced chlorosis'.

It is only recently that scientists have fully understood how alkaline-loving plants obtain iron and manganese from soils where these elements appear inaccessible. Apparently, the plants naturally secrete oxalic or citric acid in their roots – through an intimate relationship with mycorrhizal fungi in the soil (see panel). This means that the plants are in effect creating their own acidic conditions: citric acid dissolves iron and manganese, whilst oxalic acid dissolves phosphorus. The plants can then absorb these dissolved solutions as necessary.

MYCORRHIZAL FUNGI

Since the dawn of time, more than 80 per cent of the world's plants have been benefiting from a relationship with these fungi that naturally occur in the soil. Mycorrhizal fungi create a deep root system (much deeper than the plants they host with), so gaining access to many more nutrients in the lower soil levels. The fungi then release chemicals that are beneficial to the plants. It is a truly symbiotic relationship.

Mycorrhizal fungi exist naturally with plants in a well-balanced soil. However, over-cultivated plots, new building sites, new landscaping projects, and commercial potting preparations will all have reduced or damaged mycorrhizal presence.

Mycorrhizal preparations are available via mail order and from many garden centres and, as in nature, plants treated with these outperform non-treated specimens, often with remarkable results.

ABOVE **The soil at building sites is often removed or altered, so affecting the levels of micorrhizal fungi present.**

MEASURING ACIDITY AND ALKALINE CONDITIONS

Alkalinity and acidity is measured by the concentration of hydrogen ions in water, and is expressed as 'pH', or 'percentage hydrogen'.

The scale is divided from 0 to 14, including decimal placings. The 'neutral' point is pH 7.0. Figures below pH 7.0 indicate acidic conditions; the lower the figure the more acidic the soil. As far as this book is concerned, however, we are more interested in the figures above pH 7.0 which indicate alkalinity; the higher the figure the stronger the degree of alkalinity.

The pH scale is logarithmic. This means that a change of one pH unit represents a change of x10 in alkalinity; a change of 2 pH units represents a change of x100 in alkalinity, and so on. Thus the alkalinity at pH 10.0 is one thousand times the alkalinity at pH 7.0.

The following is a list of specific pH levels that may help in understanding the relevance.

You will see from this table that pH 8.5 is given as the upper limit for a chalky soil. There will be a few plants that can succeed in soil so strongly alkaline, but the vast majority of alkaline-loving plants will prefer the pH range from

ABOVE Alkaline soils over chalk and limestone bedrock are an oatmeal colour. They drain rapidly after rain and they are generally stony.

7.0–8.0. Indeed, there are many alkaline-lovers that will tolerate slightly acid conditions quite happily (see the Directory section starting on page 84).

See Chapter 2, to find out how to determine the pH level of your soil, and what the effects are of changing a pH level.

TABLE 1: Specific pH levels:

pH	
pH 13.9	Caustic soda
pH 12.4	Lime water
pH 12.0	Bleach
pH 11.0	Ammonia
pH 9.0	Antacid tablets
pH 8.5	Upper limit on chalky soil
pH 8.0	Sea water/baking soda
pH 7.0	Neutral point (also pure water, human blood and cow's milk)
pH 6.5	The ideal pH for soil (i.e. the level which suits the vast majority of plants)
pH 5.7	Saturated carbonic acid (strong acid rain)
pH 4.0 (approx)	The lower limit for most soils (also beer/coffee)
pH 3.0	Vinegar
pH 2.6	Strong lemon juice
pH 0.5	Battery acid
pH 0.1	Hydrochloric acid

HOW AN ALKALINE OR NEUTRAL SOIL CAN BECOME ACIDIC OVER TIME

Rainwater drains through a soil and gradually removes the calcium and other bases (such as the trace elements of magnesium, copper, sulphur, zinc, iron, manganese and molybdenum). When this happens, some soils become acidic. This affects medium and heavy soils less than sandy soils. Compared with heavier soils, sandy soils need only lose comparatively small quantities of lime to become extremely acid, and this loss can occur over a short space of time – even just a few years.

SOME PEATS CONTAIN LIME

Most gardeners know that if a soil is 'peaty', it is full of humus, is usually very fertile and, more appropriately here, is acidic in nature. However, in some of the world's peat reserves, including the Fenlands of Eastern England, the peat was formed in swampy areas where rivers drained through to the open sea. Many of these rivers drain from chalk hills and contain a great deal of dissolved lime. Consequently, peat from these areas is heavily charged with lime and can therefore be used to support alkaline-loving plants; indeed, it should not be used for growing acid-lovers.

Peat containing amounts of lime tends to rot rapidly when it is exposed to oxidation, so deposits can disappear relatively quickly from the landscape. By contrast, acid peat is much more stable, and resistant to decomposition.

It is entirely possible that a chalk downland, with an alkaline soil, may also bear clay caps with acid deposits which can support colonies of plants such as azaleas and camellias, that are reluctant to grow on adjacent ground.

ABOVE **When rainwater drains through a marginally alkaline soil it can gradually leach calcium and other elements over time, turning the soil acidic.**

ABOVE **Just because you may have a peat soil, it does not mean that it is necessarily highly acidic – some peat soils also contain a quantity of dissolved lime.**

CHAPTER 2

How to cope with an alkaline soil

It will be shown throughout this book that a garden on an alkaline soil can be as good as any in the land, provided gardeners stick to plants that like lime, and turn their backs on the ericaceous plants that demand an acid soil.

There are several products that make it possible to grow an occasional acid-loving plant on soil with a high chalk content but the effect is not permanent and the plant is usually never as happy as when grown on soil that is appropriate to it.

For example, some gardeners try lining with gypsum the holes in which lime-haters are to be planted. It may work for the first few months or even a year, but after this time the plant's roots penetrate further, and the effect of the gypsum is lost.

ABOVE A garden on alkaline soil can be as good as any in the land. Here we can see fine examples of pink *Phlox paniculata* 'Fairy's Petticoat' and golden yellow *Ligularia* …

ABOVE ... and stunning late-season interest with pale mauve *Aster frikartii* and yellow *Rudbeckia deamii*.

TESTING THE pH OF SOIL

Anyone who is investing in their garden, by spending money or purchasing plants, should know precisely what their soil contains. Farmers and professional growers can send soil samples away to laboratories for analysis. These tests will ascertain the pH level of the soil, but scientists will also look for presence of heavy metal content and chemical residues and some analyses will provide a breakdown of soil constituents (sand, clay, silt, loam and so on).

Home gardeners can send soil away for testing, but this is a long and expensive process. The analysis provided is likely to be far more detailed than is really necessary for a domestic garden situation, so it is easier and more appropriate to test the soil yourself.

There are several cheap amateur soil-testing kits available, and these comprise a pack of small test tubes, with colour charts and a full set of instructions. These kits vary in content and usage according to the make, but they nearly all provide some form of pH analysis. The more expensive versions will also test for nitrogen, phosphorous and potash. Some kits also include useful advice about applying fertilizer and how to alter pH. The tests take only a few minutes.

You can carry out the testing any time of year, but the most accurate readings are usually made in spring or autumn, when the soil is neither too wet nor too dry and is neither too warm nor too cold. See picture panel on page 20 to see a typical testing process.

19

USING A SOIL-TESTING KIT TO DETERMINE THE pH LEVEL

1 Soil test kits for amateurs are widely available from garden centres.

2 To test for pH levels, carefully open the capsule containing the assessment powder, and put the powder into the test tube.

3 Take a sample of soil from about 4in (10cm) below the surface.

4 Place a small amount of soil into the tube so that it sits on top of the powder.

5 Add water, preferably distilled, according to the instructions.

6 Cap the tube and shake it thoroughly.

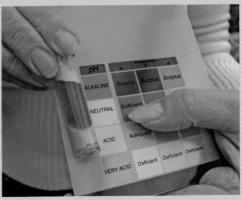

7 Allow the contents to settle, and compare against the chart. Here you can see that the soil has turned the liquid green, which clearly indicates that it is classed as alkaline to very alkaline.

IMPROVING HUNGRY ALKALINE SOILS

An alkaline soil will vary from the thin, very chalky soils of downlands, to chalky marls, which contain much fine material, and even clay; they are distinguishable from most other soils in that they are usually some shade of grey. The limestone soils produce a heavy stony loam, usually coloured from ochre to red by the presence of iron compounds.

Except for the alkaline clays the drainage is good, particularly on the chalk, and therefore such soils are naturally dry and warm. What they usually lack is humus, and therefore they are improved by the addition of manure, compost, or leafmould; these decompose very rapidly, as will be evident to anyone who has searched for leafmould in a beech wood on chalk. This means that the heaviest dressings possible are desirable on chalk soils.

As the humus content of soil increases, the colour of the soil becomes darker, as may be observed by comparing the colour of the soil in long-established gardens with the natural soil of the district.

ADJUSTING THE pH OF SOIL

Once a pH test has been conducted, you will know whether your soil is alkaline, neutral, acid or even very acid. This gives you a general indication of the sorts of plants you can grow with relative ease. Each plant species has a range of pH over which it will grow well; above or below this range it will grow poorly, or fail altogether. A slight change in the pH level may enable you to grow a much wider, and therefore more rewarding, range of plants.

Raising and lowering pH is not an exact science and most plants have a reasonably wide tolerance, certainly to within 1 pH point. Consult the Directory section of this book (on pages 84–154) and you will see that many of the plants recommended for alkaline soils will also tolerate neutral and slightly acid soils.

Altering pH takes time, so do not expect rapid changes; work steadily towards giving a plant its ideal conditions. The tables on the next few pages give approximate amounts to alter pH by 1 pH point up or down the scale. But it is important when you are attempting to alter the pH level of your soil to understand the full range of implications, over and above the alkalinity rating. For example:

Trace elements These are very sensitive to pH changes. At low pH levels they become very soluble, and toxic excesses may occur. At high pH levels (above 7.5) all the trace elements except one (molybdenum) are much less soluble, and crop deficiencies may occur.

Soil bacteria Lowering the pH level reduces the activity of nitrifying bacteria and nitrogen-fixing bacteria. Note that below pH 4.5 the activity of soil bacteria ceases (but anyone gardening on an alkaline soil is unlikely to be able to reduce the pH this far).

ABOVE **An alkaline soil can contain much fine material, and even clay.**

21

USING IRON CHELATES

There are some chemical formulations, such as iron chelates (sold as Sequestrene or Miracid) which, they claim, will enable one to grow, for instance, rhododendrons and camellias on a chalk soil. In my experience, these do work. However for anything likely to grow taller and wider than a man, say, the cost would escalate to levels where it becomes impracticable.

In my opinion plants alien to the soils in question, however dealt with, never look as happy as they do when in a more suitable environment. Using iron chelates to grow one or two of the smaller plants for which one has a special affection is another matter, and may be done at no great cost. It is important that the manufacturer's instructions are followed closely, as dosages can vary. If you marginally over- or under-supply your plants with it they are unlikely to come to long-term harm, but this does not apply to massive overdosing.

BELOW **Use iron chelates to grow favourite – and small – acid-loving plants on an alkaline soil.**

LOWERING THE pH OF VERY ALKALINE SOIL

Soil pH can be lowered by the addition of acid materials (Table 1). For example, if flowers of sulphur is added to soil it is slowly converted to sulphuric acid by soil bacteria. Also, ammonia-containing fertilizers, and in particular sulphate of ammonia, will remove lime from soil and lower soil pH.

Acid peat may be dug into the soil, and this can work extremely well, but it has little effect on heavy soils with a large lime reserve.

The pH of sandy soils may be lowered fairly easily (just as it may be easily raised with a small dressing of lime), compared with a heavy soil. It is therefore much easier to over-lime and under-lime sandy soils than heavy soils.

Dressings of organic manures or composts – or using iron chelates – will also reduce the pH levels. Grassing down an apple orchard and keeping the grass mown will help to keep the pH level lower.

TABLE 2: To increase soil acidity by 1 pH point (all soils):

	Add
Sulphate of ammonia	2oz per sq yd (70g per m^2)
Flowers of sulphur	2oz per sq yd (70g per m^2)
Peat	44oz per sq yd (1.5kg per m^2)
Compost	272oz per sq yd (9.25kg per m^2)
Manure	88oz per sq yd (3kg per m^2)

LEFT **Dressings of organic manures will, over time, reduce the pH level of soil.**

23

ABOVE In natural woodland, leaves such as beech and oak (seen here) fall to the ground. This 'litter' slowly returns goodness to the soil.

RAISING THE pH OF ACIDIC SOIL

It is entirely possible that some readers of this book are hoping to grow alkaline-loving plants even though they have an acidic soil. Also, if your soil is neutral or even slightly alkaline, you may desire to raise the pH level.

Acid rain leads to a continual loss of lime from the soil, and this is worse in some parts of the world than others, depending on the position of industrial areas in relation to the prevailing weather. It means that the soil in such areas is tending to become more acid. Less rain is needed on sandy soil for the effect to take place, than on heavy soils.

Heavier soils naturally carry a cover of broadleaved trees such as beech or oak. Deep roots from these trees absorb calcium and other bases that would otherwise be lost from the soil, and these are returned to the surface of the soil with the leaf litter that falls every autumn. In a beech wood several hundred hundredweights per acre (kilogrammes per hectare) of carbonate of lime are deposited every year in the leaf litter and this prevents the soil from becoming acid.

Liming a soil will raise the pH level. Lime is a word that is used so loosely these days that it no longer has any definite meaning. There are two principal types of liming material commonly available: ground limestone, also called ground chalk or carbonate of lime – $CaCO_3$; and hydrated lime, also known as slaked lime or calcium hydroxide – $Ca(OH)_3$.

Quicklime, also referred to as burnt lime, or calcium oxide – CaO, may also be found in some shops or mail-order suppliers, but this is not so common; if you have this to use, apply it at roughly half the rate of ground limestone.

ABOVE **Liming, if carried out evenly and carefully, will usefully raise the pH of the soil; here ground limestone is being spread.**

TABLE 3: To increase soil acidity by 1 pH point:

	Addition of ground limestone
Sandy soil	6oz per sq yd (203g per m^2)
Loam soil	9oz per sq yd (306g per m^2)
Clay soil	13oz per sq yd (443g per m^2)

	Addition of hydrated lime
Sandy soil	5oz per sq yd (170g per m^2)
Loam soil	7oz per sq yd (240g per m^2)
Clay soil	9oz per sq yd (306g per m^2)

ABOVE Leafmould, made by laying down rotted leaves, collected together and compressed over several years, is one of the best ways to add humus to the soil.

THE IMPORTANCE OF HUMUS

Adding neutral compost to an alkaline soil will slightly reduce the pH level over time. But the biggest advantage will be the improvement afforded by the compost to the soil's structure.

Humus is rotted organic matter that bulks out the soil, improving its structure and moisture retention. If the natural soil is deficient in humus it must be made good by the addition of suitable materials. This is relevant to all soils, but particularly so in the case of a sandy one. If you are growing vegetables, particularly, and regardless of the type of soil you have, you should dig it over once a year, and whenever possible incorporate plenty of humus.

Manure is better than well-rotted compost if you are wanting to feed the soil and increase its moisture-retaining capabilities; manure from pigs and horses is most commonly available, usually from farms that put up signs. Sometimes a town-based garden centre will be able to order it in for you. It is not particularly expensive but it is heavy and, although it does not prevent weed growth, it produces luxuriant plant growth. Poultry manure is also available, but this is very strong and needs to be dried out to use as a fertilizer dressing rather than manure.

LEFT Dried manure products are available these days for using as fertilizers, rather than bulky organic matter.

Do remember that compost or manure has to be well rotted as, if it rots while it is in the ground, it can deplete the soil in the immediate vicinity of much-needed nitrogen.

Work the bulky matter, which improves the soil texture and fertility, into the soil at the time of digging. The addition of such material is recommended for many soil types, including clay, where it helps to open up the sticky soil, so improving the drainage of rainwater. Conversely, organic matter also helps free-draining soils such as sands and gravels, to hold on to moisture and plant foods, since it acts like a sponge.

Organic matter is added to the trenches while digging, at a rate of at least one level barrow-load per 4sq yd (3.7m^2). Digging should be carried out regularly on the vegetable plot and on beds used for bedding plants, generally in autumn, and soil should always be dug prior to planting permanent plants (trees, shrubs, perennials and so on) and even before laying a lawn.

For other natural bulking products, which are good for incorporating into hungry soils, see those listed overleaf.

ABOVE **Animal manure – such as this horse manure – should only be added to the soil when it is well rotted. It will feed the soil and, over several years, will improve its structure immeasurably.**

RIGHT **Organic matter being added to the soil while digging. This will help retain moisture and ensure healthy plants.**

ABOVE Wood ash from bonfires and garden incinerators can also be added to compost heaps.

ABOVE If you make your own garden compost at home, and do it right, you will end up with a wonderful, friable, dark, fine material.

ABOVE Any woody material, such as hedge prunings, should be shredded finely so that it decomposes quicker and more effectively.

RECYCLING GARDEN WASTE

Another phrase for this, of course, is 'making your own compost'. But how easy is it, if you do it properly? The answer is: very!

In essence, all plants – and parts of plants – rot down to make compost. Annual plants come to the end of their lives every autumn; biennials at the end of their second year; perennials after a number of years when they've become too old or we've become fed up with them and dug them up. And then, of course, there are weeds, which can very often be pulled up and added to the compost heap whole.

There are many other items that can be added to a compost heap, including peelings and unused bits of vegetables from the kitchen, as well as grass mowings, shredded prunings and any other bits of soft, green matter. Even small amounts of paper, if shredded by an office shredder, can be added. All of these items will rot down to a fraction of their former size, and in so doing will become good, available humus in the soil. The best compost heaps contain a really diverse mixture of materials.

It is important to shred the prunings from woody shrubs and trees, as wood tends to take a long time to rot. Therefore, the smaller the bits, the quicker they'll decompose. Soft things are generally best for a compost heap, so the rule should always be: the harder the material, the smaller it should be.

And wood ash, in small quantities, is a good additive to the compost heap. Although this contains high doses of calcium, so can raise the soil pH, if you already have an alkaline soil this increase is unlikely to be significant.

Leafmould (see page 28) is another good soil conditioner. It can take as little as six weeks to make good compost, if it is in the height of summer and you add just small bits of green matter and some activator – usually a nitrogen-based substance that speeds up the rotting process. Or it can take a year or more, if there are lots of thick, dry autumn leaves, or a fair amount of shredded wood, or you started the heap in the autumn (the speed of rotting decreases in winter).

The whole aim in all of this is to produce, at the end, a wonderful, friable, dark, fine material that can be dug into the soil. If it is fine enough, it could even be used as a seed compost. Or it can be used as a mulch (see page 32).

DO NOT PUT THE FOLLOWING ON A COMPOST HEAP:

- Household plastic, silver foil, metal and glass items

- The roots of perennial weeds such as couch grass, ground elder, bindweed, docks and dandelions. These will almost certainly continue to grow and you'll probably end up spreading them around the garden

- Cooked food – meat, fish, cheese and grease. Aside from smelling bad, these things will encourage rats and other unwanted vermin.

ABOVE Mulching — here with shredded bark — helps to conserve moisture, and keeps down weeds.

WHAT IS 'MULCHING'?

This is simply a layer of organic (or inorganic) material applied around plants and on top of the soil surface. There are several benefits in putting down a 2in (5cm) layer of mulch spread over a warmed, moist soil in spring. Preventing evaporation of soil moisture is the first one. Suppressing weed growth is another (if they do seed in the mulch they are easily pulled up). And a third benefit is that the mulch will gradually add to the humus content of the soil through the action of earthworms.

Homemade composts and leafmould are the first choice for anyone who wants to maintain a good quality soil. Well-rotted farmyard manure is also excellent, but a ready supply is not so easily sourced. If applied in a raw state, their composite strength (acidic and high in ammonia) could damage the soil or any live plant material it touches. In fact, even in its well-rotted state, it should not be laid so that it touches the plants, as it will cause 'scorching'.

Bark is relatively biodegradable, cheap and light as well as having excellent moisture-retaining and weed-suppressing qualities. It is available in colours other than 'natural'. Cocoa-bean shells, coir fibre and even hair mulches are available. There are also a number of different fabric mulches for allowing rain through, but preventing (or at least reducing) water evaporation from the soil.

ABOVE Watering is more important on quick-draining alkaline soils – particularly in summer when the weather is hot and dry, and plants are in active growth.

WATERING ON AN ALKALINE SOIL

Watering in dry summers while establishing trees and shrubs is absolutely essential on limy and chalky soils. Chalk absorbs, or drains moisture quickly, so making it less accessible to the plants. The most water-efficient (and arguably the most time-efficient) way to water plants on a chalk soil is by using a drip irrigation system.

It is possible to purchase, at reasonable cost, a complete drip-irrigation system for the whole garden (or a section of it, or even just for use in a greenhouse). Pipes and branches of pipes with pre-drilled holes along their length can be laid throughout the area to be watered. They can even be sited strategically to get close to specific plants – or, more accurately, the root area of specific plants. When they are connected to a tap and it is turned on, the water seeps out of the holes and soaks the immediate area.

This type of system is generally very efficient in its use of water, but it can lead to a high percentage of evaporation if the water drips on to soil in full sun, especially if the soil is compacted and the water is not absorbed readily. However, you can negate this by activating the system to come on at night by using a timer device.

Control is essential if water is not to be wasted. Whether the drip system is fitted to the mains water supply or to a rainwater storage tank, it is all too easy to leave on the tap by accident, with the subsequent waste of water. It is useful, therefore, to purchase a timer-controlled water valve, which enables a regular watering scheme to be established. This must be monitored, however, as watering requirements will vary with the seasons and weather conditions.

CHAPTER 3

How to design a garden on chalky soil

There is so much more to the world of 'gardening on chalk' than merely avoiding growing rhododendrons and heathers (the archetypal 'ericaceous', or acid-loving plants). But, as with creating a garden on acidic clay, silt or sand, it is a matter of choosing the right plants and incorporating them so that they develop in the optimum and most attractive ways. Once you know your soil type, you can plan accordingly.

ABOVE *Robinia pseudoacacia* 'Frisia' AGM makes a lovely garden tree and tolerates alkaline soil.

ABOVE *Fagus sylvatica* 'Purpurea Nana' is a good copper-leaved form of beech which, if trimmed, makes a good garden plant.

STARTING WITH A CLEAN SHEET

If you are lucky enough to move to a garden on alkaline soil that is bare – perhaps left fresh after the builders have gone, or the garden is just laid down to grass – then you will have a wealth of design options available to you.

However, the first job should be to record the garden on paper. If you are planning beds, borders, lawn, patio/deck, and possibly things like a pond or shed then it is best if you produce a scale drawing or plan of the area. This must include all of the garden's 'fixtures and fittings', i.e. the house, greenhouse/conservatory, immovable and desirable trees and shrubs, the driveway, paving and walling, drains, electricity poles, sewers and sumps.

You will need to conduct your own 'survey' of the garden. Walk around the house (and any fixed outbuildings) and make a large sketch of the layout, in plan form but not necessarily to scale. A long, flexible measuring tape is useful. The back door, or some other fixed part of the property, is a good starting point.

The ideal places for the most important elements of your future garden (patio, lawn, greenhouse, vegetable garden and so on as appropriate) should be marked on the plan. The remaining spaces will be left for you to put in your favourite alkaline-loving plants.

ABOVE **If you are planning a new layout for your garden, or a part of it, it is best to produce a scale drawing or plan first.**

ABOVE *Prunus pendula*, one of the flowering cherries, will grow well on an alkaline soil.

TREES

These are the 'backbone' of any good garden, and they are a real, long-term investment. They can be, and should be, viewed from all sides. They can be used to hide an eyesore such as a telegraph pole or electricity pylon, and they make a focal point.

Trees can be grown for a number of other gardening reasons, too. They can create and cast shade, they can be grown for their leaves, flowers, fruits and bark; some people even grow them for their attractive winter outlines. Plenty of birds will be attracted if there are trees about – for perching, roosting and for food (a tree has unseen and untold thousands of insects all over it).

It is a fact of life that trees outlive us. Our ancestors, who could only have imagined what the eventual appearance of them would be, planted the mature trees of today. You should not concern yourself, however, with the thought that a tree you plant this year may not reach its optimum height and beauty until after you have gone. Think of the next few generations, and how they will thank you for your actions.

It should be noted that most trees, even if content on a thin, chalky topsoil, do not reach the height that they would in richer conditions. But there are exceptions, and a few trees will come close to their counterparts on a benign neutral soil.

The best example of this is the beech (*Fagus sylvatica*). This can attain huge proportions and is better thought of as a parkland tree. Smaller forms are available, and young plants can be trimmed into hedges for medium-sized gardens. There are also some lovely dark, copper-coloured forms.

The walnut (forms of *Juglans*) can survive happily on a dry, thin soil, and may actually do better here than on a rich soil, because in the latter it can grow too quickly and lushly. When this happens the young branches can be snapped in high wind.

Both of these are large trees but, of the more garden-sized trees, the mostly widely grown on alkaline soils must be the flowering cherry (forms of *Prunus*). A great many more trees, including many conifers, will thrive with their feet in a chalky soil (see pages 119–144).

SHRUBS

Because their roots are not so demanding of depth, vast numbers of shrubs can tolerate thin, chalky soil. Whereas trees are the backbone, shrubs form the 'muscle' of the garden. The word 'shrub' derives from the Low German *shrubben*, meaning coarse and uneven. In Old English the word became *scrybb*. Both these old words conjure images of scrub, a word itself used to define bushes randomly growing. In a garden, however, shrubs play a hugely important role.

It is perfectly possible to have shrubs in flower throughout the year – even in the depths of winter, when blooms are particularly welcome to brighten up the garden. There are shrubs with fragrant flowers, shrubs with golden evergreen leaves, shrubs with fiery autumn colours, shrubs with berries and shrubs with attractive bark.

In design terms, fragrant shrubs should always be sited where they can be sniffed at close range; thorny shrubs should always be planted so that their branches do not rip clothing if you walk past them; and in shrub borders the tallest ones go at the back whilst the smaller ones go at the front (in an 'island' bed set within a lawn, the tallest shrubs should be in the centre, with progressively smaller ones towards the edges). Other than these three fundamentals, shrubs can more or less go anywhere.

The limitations will be determined by the ultimate size of a given shrub and whether or not it is appropriate to the space you are offering it, the hardiness of the shrub – some are sub-tropical and tender whilst others can withstand arctic conditions – and ultimately, of course, the type of soil you have.

ABOVE *Caryopteris* x *clandonensis* 'Arthur Simmonds' AGM: one of the many shrubs suited to alkaline soils.

ABOVE *Weigela* 'Florida Variegata' AGM boasts attractive flowers and foliage, and has a liking for a chalky soil.

CLIMBERS AND WALL SHRUBS

There will always be a side, back or front of a house that cries out for plant cover. Every garden wall and fence offers an opportunity for plant growth. So how can a gardener make the most of these spots?

Today, garden sizes are getting smaller and smaller and we frequently have to pick and choose our plants with care, to avoid the problem of them outgrowing the spaces we have allotted them. One way to increase the plant quotient in a small garden is to grow 'upwards', and more and more gardeners are clothing their house walls and garden fences, as well as the ground, with colour and foliage.

Of course there are many other ways to grow climbers: some will grow happily through trees and large shrubs; others will ramble over a garage or shed roof, and yet more can be grown in borders and trained to grow over trellis panels, frames and obelisks.

ABOVE *Solanum crispum* 'Glasnevin' AGM is not a true climbing plant, but should only be grown next to a wall – and preferably in an alkaline soil.

ABOVE *Ceanothus* (this is the cultivar 'Blue Mound' AGM) are perfect shrubs for growing in a sheltered spot under a sunny wall.

Interestingly, there are some types of garden shrub that do not fair too well on alkaline soils (many forms of *Hydrangea* for example), yet a climbing version, such as *Hydrangea anomala* subsp. *petiolaris* AGM will romp away on chalk. This is also the case with some roses – the hybrid tea rose 'Madame Caroline Testout', for example will probably languish and steadily decline on chalk, but its vertical version 'Climbing Madame Caroline Testout' will flourish.

Suitable climbing plants for a chalk soil include forms of *Lonicera*, *Passiflora*, *Wisteria* and some *Clematis*.

Wall shrubs are different to climbers, in that they do not naturally climb, yet they are best planted next to a wall. This may be because they prefer to take advantage of the shelter the wall offers, or they prefer the drier soil conditions that inevitably exist in the lee of a wall.

Many such shrubs can be grown freestanding, but sometimes there can be a benefit in tying some of the stems to wires stretched across the wall, as this supports and 'anchors' the plant which, if it is shallow-rooting, will give it purpose.

Typical wall shrubs for an alkaline soil include forms of *Ceanothus*, *Carpenteria*, *Chaenomeles*, *Cotoneaster horizontalis*, *Fremontodendron*, *Garrya*, *Jasminum nudiflorum*, *Phygelius*, *Pyracantha* and forms of *Solanum crispum*.

MIXED BORDERS AND BEDS

A hundred years ago we had what were called 'herbaceous borders', which contained mainly herbaceous plants, but this is actually a misnomer as all non-woody, flowering plants are, technically, herbaceous. Today we don't use the term 'herbaceous plant' in the way that the Victorians referred to them; instead we call them more correctly perennials, annuals, biennials or bulbous plants. And these all go into what we today refer to as mixed borders. Mixed borders can also be the home to some shrubs, bulbs, roses, a hedge backdrop and even a small tree if there is room.

Perennials: There are many excellent perennials that enjoy life on alkaline soil. Some, such as forms of *Paeonia*, like to be planted with a rich soil mixture but then, once established, are happy to produce their optimum displays with a fairly lean, impoverished soil.

However, some perennials on chalk grow without the intense flower colouring they would have if grown in a more neutral soil. One example of a plant – albeit a shrub – producing a different-coloured flower as a result of the soil pH is that of the mophead hydrangea. Flowers may be bright blue on an acid soil, but a muddy mauve on an alkaline soil. It desperately wants to be pink, like many of its closely-related hybrids and cultivars, but its 'blue genes' are preventing it. On acid and neutral soil it can be a clear and vivid blue. On chalky soil the flowerheads might be a muddy pink-mauve. Similarly the perennial Himalayan poppy (*Meconopsis betonicifolia*) changes from being a bright blue on an acid soil, to an almost lavender colour on chalk. On the plus side, the best *Salvia patens* I ever grew was on a chalky soil – its blue colour was so intense it was almost mesmerizing.

ABOVE **Summer bedding schemes are usually bright and garish, and an alkaline soil can be every bit as colourful as an acid one.**

It is a curious twist of fate that annual and perennial *Gypsophila* does not always flourish on a chalky soil. In fact, it has a recommended pH value of 6.0–7.5, which is most definitely in the neutral range and, if anything, leaning more towards the acidic. However, the name when translated from the Greek *gypsos* and *philos* means 'lover of chalk'!

As with shrubs in beds and borders, the tallest perennials go at the back, or in the centre.

ABOVE A *Hosta* grown in a container can be moved to a more prominent position when it is looking its best and, if situated on 'pot feet', it may even be more resistant to attack by slugs in a pot.

ABOVE Containers permanently planted with shrubs – such as *Choisya ternata* 'Sundance' AGM – look good all year round.

RAISED BEDS

Generally, I believe that raised beds are an important aspect of a garden. They can be edged with ornamental stone, concrete blocks, bricks, or even old railway sleepers (available from specialist suppliers, usually listed in your local telephone directory).

The side wall of a raised bed, unlike a tall brick wall or the side of a building, does not usually need footings, or a foundation. However, these structures do retain an often heavy bank of soil, and you do not want them to collapse under the pressure. When I have constructed these in the past I have dug a trench – some 4in (10cm) deep – along the line where the wall will be, and into this trench I have poured a cement/concrete ready-mix. Smooth the surface, then water it lightly with a rosed watering can and leave it overnight. The next day you will have a sturdy base, bonded to the surrounding soil, on to which you can build your retaining wall. With this kind of footing, however, the wall should be no more than four courses high.

Both bulbous and alpine plants are most ideally suited to raised beds, but both types of plant insist on good drainage, and you should add extra coarse sand or grit into planting holes. The higher plants should be towards the centre of the bed, with the lower ones at the front and do not, of course, forget to grow a few trailing plants to hang down the sides.

PLANTS IN CONTAINERS

Every gardener, regardless of their soil, should grow plants in containers. Vases, troughs, pots, tubs, urns, hanging baskets, windowboxes and even growing bags can be used, and the benefit for those of us with a strongly alkaline (or strongly acidic) soil is that, by choosing compost mixtures with a markedly different pH, you will be able to grow some different plants in the containers to those that may be grown in the garden.

ABOVE **Special hollow bulb-planter tools are available for using on grass and naturalized areas.**

Tulips do not need to be planted until late autumn, as they produce their roots late. The majority of bulbs can be planted as soon as the summer bedding has been removed, or when the ground is vacant.

Most gardeners use a simple trowel, however there are special graduated bulb-planting trowels available; these have a long narrow blade with measurements marked on, making it easier to determine the correct depth. If you are planting bulbs in grass a hand-held bulb planter is helpful, as it removes a plug of soil when pushed into the ground. The bulb is inserted and the plug replaced; it is a much quicker method when large numbers are involved. When planting, ensure the base of the bulb is in contact with the ground, as air pockets result in the roots failing to develop. However, this is not practicable if you have vast numbers of bulbs to plant. Here it is just as effective, much easier and less time consuming, to slice off a patch of turf with a spade, slip in a handful of bulbs and then replace the turf, firming it with your foot. It may seem like a 'rough and ready' way of doing things, but it does work well.

Annuals and biennials: Be careful that you do not plant tender annuals outdoors before they are ready, as cold weather will kill them off, or cause irreparable damage to them. These plants, which will have been started into growth in a greenhouse, will need very slow acclimatization in spring to colder conditions – a term known as 'hardening off'. They should not be fully planted out in the garden or in containers until all danger of frost is over.

Before putting them out fork the soil over, making sure that any annual weeds are completely buried, and perennial weeds (with thicker, lusher roots) are removed as, if left, these will re-grow. Then apply a sprinkling of general fertilizer evenly over the soil, following the manufacturer's instructions.

Give the plants a thorough watering an hour or two before planting them, so that they are not stressed prior to the move. Gently take the young plants out of their pots, or remove them singly from their trays or polystyrene strips.

ABOVE **Do not be in a rush to plant out young annuals and bedding plants. If they go out too early, before the weather warms up, they could perish.**

ABOVE **When planting bedding plants make sure they are firmed in position well, but not so much that you damage the roots.**

ABOVE **Like outdoor plants, house plants can have a preference for a particular kind of soil – every home should have a few, as they engender wellbeing.**

Place the bedding plants in holes, dug with a trowel, which are the same size as the pot. Firm them in place gently and then water them.

I cannot stress too highly the care that should be taken when planting annuals and biennials: damaged leaves will be replaced with new leaves, within reason, but a plant only has one stem, so avoid causing it any damage.

HOUSE AND CONSERVATORY PLANTS

It is not just outdoor plants that prefer acid or alkaline soils – indoor and greenhouse plants are just as demanding; but, because we nearly always grow them in containers, and either keep them in the pots that they arrived in or re-pot them using multi-purpose bagged compost, we don't think so much about their soil needs.

Any bright room can be host to a selection of house plants, and the brighter the room, the more choice you have. For example, a conservatory gives us the best opportunity as it provides copious amounts of daylight, the lack of which can sometimes be the death knell of some indoor plants. If all you can offer in terms of space is a dark hallway or bathroom with no natural light, you will probably be able to grow a fern or two, but little else.

Which indoor plants are alkaline-lovers? The maidenhair fern (*Adiantum*), hart's tongue fern (*Asplenium*), pelargonium, cherry pie (*Heliotropum*) and *Hibiscus* all require alkaline soils if they are to do well. See the A–Z Directory (pages 150–154) for more details and descriptions

FRUITS AND VEGETABLES

If you want to grow your own food, and you have an alkaline soil, don't worry. There are many types that tolerate – and even prefer – chalky conditions. And don't forget, if you want to grow something that prefers an acid soil, fortunately most food crops can also be grown in large tubs and containers with imported soil.

Vegetable crops preferring alkaline soil to a greater or lesser extent include asparagus, beans (all forms), cabbage, Brussels sprouts, beetroot, calabrese, cauliflower, Chinese cabbage, cucumber, garlic, kohlrabi, leek, marrow, mushrooms, parsnip, pumpkin, spinach, sweet corn, tomatoes and watercress. Alkaline-loving fruits include avocados, cherries, black currants, white currants, damsons, mulberries, nectarine, peach, pear, plum, quince and strawberry. Herbs generally prefer acidic conditions, but marjoram (oregano) is certainly better when grown on an alkaline soil (see A–Z Directory, pages 145–149).

ABOVE **Cherries, and most other 'stone' fruits, usually grow well on alkaline soil.**

ABOVE **Leeks, members of the onion family, enjoy alkaline soils up to around pH8.0.**

ABOVE **When planting out young vegetable plants, make sure they are firmed in well and watered. Taller kinds, such as tomatoes, may also need staking and it is best to put these in at the same time.**

CHAPTER 5

Essential maintenance

Unless you intend to have an entirely natural garden, with plants – and weeds – running amok, then you will need to offer your plants a degree of care and attention over the years. Certainly this is the case if you want them to give the best displays. Any maintenance programme can be split into five basic divisions: watering, feeding, weeding, pruning and plant problems (pests, diseases and other disorders).

ABOVE **A decorative, well-ordered garden such as this does not look after itself. Weeds and plant problems need to be controlled, and regular watering, feeding and pruning should take place.**

WATERING

Ninety per cent or more of a soft, herbaceous (that is, a non-woody) plant may consist of water, and it is water which keeps the soft young cells in the leaves and stems plump and extended. If water is in short supply, however, this cell turgidity is lost, which causes the plants' stems to become limp, and the leaves to droop and wilt. And if the water shortage is prolonged, the plant will die.

All plants need water to survive – and grow – and it is important never to allow them to dry out completely. Even the cacti found in deserts across the world need water to survive: they take in what little moisture is available and they store it within the flesh of the plant, to use when times get hard.

It is arguably even more important to attend to watering if you have a chalky soil, as this can drain so quickly (unless you have a heavy, alkaline clay). So, after you have planted up your alkaline-soil garden, it is important to water the plants regularly, until they have become established, which could take two or even three years. After this time you should continue to water your plants during hot and dry weather.

Avoid watering in the heat of the day; it is best to carry out the watering either early in the day or in the evening, as these are times when evaporation will be at its slowest. A good soaking of the soil every few days is better for plants – and less wasteful of water – than a mere splash around the leaves and stems once or twice a day. But beware: don't oversupply; too much water in the soil can be bad for plants, because the excess water replaces air and the roots become waterlogged, essentially meaning that they are being starved of oxygen.

ABOVE **Early morning and evening – away from the heat of the day – are the best times to water the garden.**

ABOVE **Alkaline soils have a tendency to dry out rapidly, so particular attention should be paid to watering.**

53

FEEDING

To discuss the feeding of plants in a general sense is difficult as there are so many variables. For example, you may be growing very 'hungry' plants, such as intensely flowering bedding plants, or food crops such as tomatoes, runner beans and strawberries. You will need to feed these with specific products several times throughout the season. Or you may live on a very fertile soil, and grow mainly slow-growing shrubs and conifers. Here the feeding regime will be merely to 'top-up' what is already in the soil, perhaps once a year. Also, plants grown directly in the ground will require less feeding than those growing in pots or containers.

Plants growing on an alkaline soil, especially if it is sandy, gritty and free-draining, are likely to need more feeding than those growing on heavier clay soils.

Undoubtedly the best way to provide your plants with good, all-round nutrition is to apply annual mulches of manure in early spring; these will help to retain moisture in the soil. Between mulches it is a good idea to supplement the feeding by applying liquid, granular or pelleted fertilizer. This is now where many gardeners – even quite experienced ones – can be easily confused, as there are so many options. In the end, the choice of fertilizer has to be yours, and dependent on which plants you have, what the feeding needs are and also the depth of your pocket.

ABOVE **There are many different products available for feeding plants, but dry, granular feeds are the most convenient to use if time is short.**

ESSENTIAL ELEMENTS

If they do not have access to any of the following 15 elements, plants will perform poorly, become susceptible to all kinds of pests and diseases or, in extreme cases, fade and die:

- Carbon, oxygen, hydrogen (all three of which are obtained from the air and water in the soil)

- Nitrogen, potassium and phosphorous (obtained from fertilizers)

- The 'trace elements', which may actually be lacking in some gardens, causing plants to go yellow, become stunted, or be flowerless. These are (again in order of importance) calcium, magnesium, sulphur, sodium, iron, manganese, zinc, copper and, finally, molybdenum.

Fertilizers labelled as 'balanced' or 'general' contain roughly equal proportions of nitrogen, phosphates and potash, and are of use to all plants. The high-potash types (including most rose and tomato fertilizers) boost flower and fruit growth, and high-nitrogen types assist the growth of foliage – important in the case of variegated plants and leaf vegetables. It is advisable to follow a programme of applying these general fertilizers during the year. You need only apply the trace element fertilizers if you have identified that your soil is lacking one or more of those lesser nutrients.

Feed plants when they are actively growing. If you feed outdoor plants when they are growing very slowly, or completely dormant, the rains will wash most of the fertilizer away.

ORGANIC FERTILIZERS

Some fertilizers are labelled 'organic' (i.e. derived from plant or animal remains). Naturally occurring minerals – although not organic – are usually also acceptable in organic food production. Chemical (or inorganic) fertilizers are man-made and usually contain higher nutrient levels, which are quickly released into moist soil. Organic fertilizers usually contain fewer plant nutrients; these are released slowly into the soil over a long period as the organic material breaks down, so there is less risk of over-feeding delicate plants.

ABOVE: **Many plants may be fed with liquid fertilizers. These are relatively fast-acting, and come in a concentrated form for diluting in a watering can.**

ABOVE Although groundsel is an annual weed, it will germinate, grow and even flower throughout the winter period.

ABOVE The best way to control weeds is by hand-weeding, but you should endeavour to dig out as much of the root as possible.

WEEDING

Weeds compete with the garden plants for moisture, nutriment, sunlight, air and space. Many weeds also harbour pests and diseases. Being much more numerous than garden plants, and frequently much more vigorous, too, it is only a short time before they can completely smother them, unless they are removed.

Action must be taken early (before weeds get too large or flower), and it must never cease (for some weeds, such as groundsel, grow, flower and set seed even in winter). The easiest weeds to control are annuals, which are best kept in check by hoeing, mulching and spraying. The more troublesome weeds, however, are the perennial weeds, such as ground elder, couch grass (or twitch), bindweed, docks, thistles and perennial nettles. These will all come up year after year if left to their own devices.

When you are first setting out plants in your alkaline soil, you should make sure that the ground is completely weed-free. If you have an area covered with, for example, bindweed, the best course of action is to spray the area with a herbicide based on glyphosate, which will kill all parts of the plant it is sprayed on to. It becomes inactive on contact with the soil, and it is not taken up by the roots of any plant, no matter how close to the area of spray. Don't pull up the weeds immediately after they have been sprayed, as this will negate the application of the chemical; wait until the plants have turned brown and wither, as you know then that the chemical has done its job. This process may take a day or two if the weather is hot and sunny, or longer if it is cool and cloudy.

To control new weed seedlings from appearing you can use a product based on simazine. The chemical acts as a sort of sealant over the soil, preventing weed seeds from germinating. Apply it in spring, when the soil is firm and moist, and it should remain active for the whole growing season.

Before applying, remove any weeds by hand. Or, if they are very small, hoe lightly. Do whatever other cultivation you need to do on the soil, such as feeding or pruning plants. Only then should you apply the simazine-based control.

Don't walk on the soil after this has been applied, as you will break the 'seal' that it provides. Ideally, finish the whole process off by applying a mulch (see below).

The best way to control perennial weeds is by hand-weeding, digging out as much of the root as possible. This is certainly the case with the deeper-rooting weeds, which may not be checked sufficiently by chemical weedkillers.

However, if the area of weed cover is large, or the weeds are growing in between difficult plants, such as those with spikes or thorns – roses, pyracanthas, hollies and so on – you could spray with a weedkiller based on dichlobenil, which will also control germinating weed seedlings and established annual weeds for up to six months after application. Apply it when the soil is moist and, preferably, in early spring before there is too much surrounding leaf cover.

If grass weeds are your main problem, apply a weedkiller based on alloxydim-sodium. It is foliage-acting, non-residual and harmless to non-grassy plants, so it will not matter if you inadvertently get some on your woody plants.

Mulching is always to be recommended. It helps to prevent weed growth (as well as retain soil moisture and generally benefits the structure of the soil over time).

But purely for weed control and moisture retention there are fabric mulches available, generally in black, brown or white. They are not designed to look particularly attractive, so they are almost always used in a kitchen garden where the aesthetics are not so important.

ABOVE **The easiest weeds to control are annuals, which are best kept in check by hoeing.**

ABOVE **Fabric mulches are effective in controlling weed growth, and retaining soil moisture, but they are not aesthetically pleasing.**

ABOVE **When pruning it is important to cut out crossing branches, as these rub up against each other and cause bad abrasions which can allow the entry of pests and diseases into the wood.**

ABOVE **Pruning a hybrid tea or floribunda rose is the epitome of pruning to promote flowering – without an annual cut-back the blooms would be smaller and less impactful.**

PRUNING

We prune plants to keep them to size, maintain their shape, improve flowering and therefore fruiting, to improve foliage and stems, and to remove unwanted growth. Generally speaking, the right time for pruning is after flowering or after the effect required.

General pruning advice is to first cut out any branches that are diseased, damaged or crossing and rubbing against other branches. Then, in the case of mature plants, cut back three or four old stems to ground level to encourage further shoots, and trim back some of the longest stems.

If a plant has got totally out of hand, cut some of the stems to ground level and the rest by a third of their length. The following year cut back the remaining stems by a third of their length also. Do this each year until the plant is of the size and shape required.

It is not a disaster if, for reasons beyond your control, shrubs are not pruned for a year or two, or even three. In time the flowers will almost certainly become smaller, even though there may be more of them; the effect will not be so good. However, in most cases shrubs will respond to pruning after this time, and it will be possible to bring them back under control.

WHEN TO PRUNE
- In the case of winter-flowering shrubs, and those that flower before mid-summer, prune immediately after flowering has finished (whenever that may be).
- With shrubs flowering after mid-summer, prune after they have got through the winter, on a mild day in spring.
- With shrubs grown for their autumn berries, it is usually best to prune them in early spring.

PLANT PROBLEMS

Alkaline-loving plants are prone to just the same sorts of problems as plants growing in any other kind of soil. But a chalk soil does cause a specific problem to a specific range of plants.

Iron deficiency The most often-seen problem affecting plants growing on an alkaline soil is that of iron deficiency (also known as lime-induced chlorosis). This affects acid-loving plants, but nearly every gardener on an alkaline soil will have (by default or design) at least a couple of plants that prefer an acid soil. And the gardener may have been wondering why these plants are persistently sickly.

In affected plants there is a yellowing of the leaves, or chlorosis, often combined with the development of brown areas of discolouration, which starts at the leaf margins and then spreads between the veins. Younger growth is usually affected earlier and more severely than older growth. The cause is simply that acid-lovers have roots that are poorly adapted for the absorption of necessary trace elements from an alkaline soil. If the soil is too alkaline, the plants develop deficiency symptoms, in particular that of iron and manganese.

Apart from avoiding growing such plants, you can treat those already there and affected, with Sequestrene or other chelated compounds containing iron, manganese and other trace elements. Use also acidic mulches, such as chopped, composted bracken or conifer bark. And finally, feed plants with an ericaceous fertilizer, that is formulated for use on acid-loving plants.

ABOVE **This acid-loving *Camellia* has been grown on an alkaline soil, which has caused it to become chlorotic, and susceptible to other disorders.**

ABOVE **Pruning will remove wayward branches, and gives you the opportunity to balance a lopsided plant.**

ABOVE Dryness at the roots can cause a plant to wilt, but a prolonged drought can cause the death of the plant.

Drought: This is not, of course, specific to alkaline soil. It can happen anywhere and at any time. However, if there is a drought, it is plants growing on thin, chalky soils (as well as quick-draining sandy soils) that are likely to suffer first. Symptoms vary depending on the plant, and even whether the drought is occasional or has been recurrent. Common symptoms include poor growth and stunting, wilting of the leaves and, in extreme cases, of flowers, stems and flower stalks. Prolonged drought may also cause buds, flowers and fruits to drop, as well as the formation of smaller fruits.

Unfortunately if a drought suddenly ends with significant watering or rainfall, the whole problem can be exacerbated because the quick intake of moisture can cause splitting or cracking of fruits and stems. The way to avoid the effects of drought is to ensure that the soil never dries out completely.

Improve the soil's moisture retention ability by incorporating bulky organic materials, such as compost, into thin, chalky and sandy soils. Apply a mulch.

Plants growing in containers should be watered even more frequently than plants in the ground and, where feasible, moved during a drought so that they are protected from the effects of direct sunlight.

There are also other problems, caused by diseases and insect and mammal pests, to which our alkaline-loving plants are susceptible.

PLANT DISEASES

These fall into three different categories: fungal, viral and bacterial. It is the first, by far, that is the most troublesome.

Fungus: Spores of a fungus can travel across the garden carried on the wind, through the soil, or via water flow. The biological aim for these spores is to settle and infect new areas. Coral spot, for example, is a disease which affects dead wood, and spreads to living wood; the coral pink round pustules, which grow on the surface of the bark, are actually quite decorative. It is spread mainly by water splashes caused by rain or irrigation.

Another example is that of honey fungus, a disease that can kill even mature trees and shrubs; it shows a white 'mycelium', a thread-like mass of filaments or strands forming the vegetative part of the fungus.

Mildew is probably the most widespread fungal disease of garden plants. It is recognized by a white, powder-like coating on leaves. 'Powdery mildew' attacks mainly the tender, younger shoots.

Without treatment, the disease will cause the affected parts to become stunted and distorted. Spores are carried on the wind, and they will most readily infect plants that are slightly dehydrated, or where there is poor air circulation around the plant, such as with climbers growing against walls. The spores germinate most readily in cool, wet weather. Of lesser importance is 'downy mildew', which is characterized by greyish-brown pustules on the undersides of the leaves.

Both of these mildews can be controlled by preventative spraying using a suitable fungicide – it will be too late if you wait until you see the presence of the disease.

ABOVE **The coral spot fungus, although quite attractive in its own right, is a disease that spreads from dead wood to living wood.**

ABOVE **Mildew, here on a *Dahlia* plant, is probably the most widespread fungal disease of garden plants.**

ABOVE Rust, a fungal disease that produces irregular discolouration on leaves and often stems, can sometimes be controlled with sprays, but you will need to act quickly.

Rust disease produces vaguely circular discolouration on leaves, corresponding loosely to dark orange, brown, yellow, or red spots or pustules on the undersides of the leaves. Stems may also be affected. Rust affects a wide variety of plants and some of the most severely affected are roses, chrysanthemums, pelargoniums, antirrhinums and hollyhocks, and even vegetables such as broad beans. Chemical sprays are available, but severely infected plants should be lifted and burnt.

Virus: Plant viruses cannot be cured. Pests – particularly greenfly and eelworms – frequently spread viruses between plants, which is why it is so important to control these insects (see below). Once infection occurs nearly every cell of a diseased plant becomes infected, and there is no method by which a gardener can cure it. The plant should destroyed – preferably by burning – as this gets rid of the virus; simply putting it on the compost heap is likely to spread the problem.

Bacteria: Infection usually enters a plant through a wound or opening. 'Bacterial canker' is a serious disease of many forms of tree and shrub, as well as fruiting plants and even vegetables such as tomatoes and cucumbers. In woody plants symptoms include oozing gum from the bark.

Several bacterial 'spots' and 'rots' also affect a range of plants. As with the viruses there is no cure, and the individual plants may need to be destroyed. In the case of trees and shrubs, it may be possible to cut out the affected parts and to seal over the wounds with protective sealants, but there is no guarantee of success.

ABOVE Blackfly, here on golden-leaved mock orange (*Philadelphus*), are relatively easily controlled with organic and chemical sprays.

INSECT PESTS
The following are the most common:

Aphids: These are the sap-sucking greenfly and blackfly that infest a wide range of plants. They feed on young, tender shoots, and are often seen clustering on young, unopened buds and on the undersides of young leaves. Their feeding will not kill an established plant, unless it is very small, but the buds and leaves will be distorted. And the potential for flowers and fruits will be reduced significantly. They can also spread diseases and viruses.

Cut off and discard small infestations. Larger infestations can be sprayed: there are a number of appropriate insecticides, some approved for organic gardeners. Always follow the manufacturers' instructions.

Red spider mites: Attacks from this pest are worst when the plants are hot, dry and under a degree of stress, which can occur readily on quick-draining chalky soils. These pests attack the leaves and stems of a wide range of plants, causing bronze patches to appear on the upper surfaces of leaves. There will probably be very fine, silky webbing between the leaves and stems. The spiders are tiny and yellowish rather than red. Chemical control is possible.

Vine weevils: Usually more troublesome on an alkaline soil, it is mainly a pest of plants growing in large tubs and containers (although it is known to affect garden plants as well). The grubs eat into the roots, causing plants to wilt and die in the period between autumn and spring. The adult weevils are active – and laying eggs – in summer, when they will eat irregular-shaped holes in leaf margins. The main control available is a chemical called imidacloprid, which is available in various formulations as a preventative, for spraying onto plants, or already impregnated in potting compost.

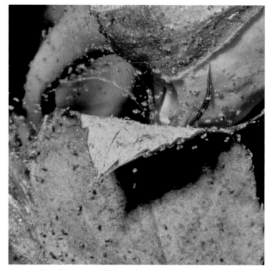

ABOVE **Red spider mites – little spiders that are rather more yellow than red – produce very fine webbing in plant crevices; the pest is more troublesome in hot, dry weather.**

ABOVE **The grub, or larva, of the vine weevil is just ¼–⅓in (6–8cm) long, but can eat roots and tubers of plants, causing considerable devastation.**

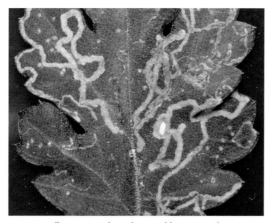

ABOVE **Caterpillars are not always large and hairy. Some burrow into the plants and are hidden from view. Leaf miner caterpillars on these *Chrysanthemum* leaves have caused tunnels and 'galleries', ruining the look of the foliage.**

ABOVE **Snails like to hide in cool, damp, shady places, such as behind containers. This colony of snails was discovered when a plant trough was moved away from a wall.**

Caterpillars: These are the larval stage of butterflies and moths. There is much variety in their size, colour and degree of hairiness, but they all have generally tubular-shaped bodies with distinct heads. They have three pairs of jointed legs at the head end and two to five pairs of clasping legs on their abdomen.

Most pest species will readily devour foliage. Others live in the soil and feed on roots, or bore into stems. Some feed on the inside of leaves – and these are referred to as leaf miners – whilst yet others feed on fruits, berries and seeds. Many feed after dark and are easier to find by torchlight on mild evenings. If they are not too numerous, pick them off by hand. Otherwise, spray with a suitable insecticide, such as those containing pyrethrum or bifenthrin, when signs of caterpillar feeding are seen.

NON-INSECT PESTS

These will vary from gastropods (slugs and snails), to four-legged creatures such as deer, badgers and foxes. But birds and certain other two-legged creatures can also be a problem.

Slugs and snails: Slugs frequently rank as the number one pest for gardeners, and several species occur in gardens. They can damage a wide range of plants and are present throughout the year, often continuing to feed in the winter if temperatures are above 5°C (40°F). Irregular holes are eaten in foliage, flowers and stems. They are usually most active after dark.

LEFT **Commonly available blue and green bait poisons will control slugs – and snails – but there are also a number of organic options, the latest being nematodes which you apply to the soil; they enter the slugs and kill them from within.**

The snail has a hard shell, but otherwise is as troublesome. In fact, snails can be more numerous in areas with alkaline soils, which naturally contain a higher proportion of the calcium salts necessary to form a shell.

Both molluscs inhabit dark, cool, moist places such as under pots or stones. They can never be eliminated from gardens, so control measures should be concentrated on protecting vulnerable plants, such as seedlings and soft new growth on perennials, bedding plants and certain vegetable crops. Slug pellets based on metaldehyde or ferric phosphate can be applied in small quantities to the ground near to susceptible plants.

I prefer to use less toxic remedies. I have tried the old wives' tales of putting down orange peel (which attracts them in numbers where they can be collected and disposed of in a manner of your choosing), and also beer traps, where they are attracted by the smell to a jar half-filled with beer, and they fall in and drown.

I have also tried the biological controls – nematodes that come dry in packets, and which you water onto the soil. This tends to afford good control for about six weeks or so, and then needs to be reapplied. It is arguably better for controlling the underground slugs that usually target bulbs and potato tubers.

Birds: Many birds will eat the berries and other fruits from ornamental and productive trees and shrubs. For example, wood pigeons and blackbirds can strip a holly tree of berries in a matter of a few hours. Other birds break in to ripening apples and pears hanging on the trees, while others eat flower buds just before they burst open.

Netting – either draped over vulnerable plants, or in the form of a structured 'fruit cage' – is the only guaranteed way to control them. A purpose-built fruit cage can work wonders for productive fruit canes, bushes and small trees. Bird scarers, made from shiny or glittering items hung amongst the branches of susceptible trees and bushes, work only with mixed success.

BELOW **Feeding garden birds can help to save desirable berries, seedheads and buds on garden plants from being eaten.**

I believe, however, that we should encourage birds into our gardens, as some – most notably thrushes – will eat slugs and snails. Others (including many members of the sparrow and tit families) consume vast quantities of aphids and other small crawlers. Actively feeding the birds can actually help, in a small way, to save precious berries and other plant features from the ravages of birds – but barrier controls of netting are still to be recommended where valuable crops of fruit and vegetables are concerned.

Mammals The worst offenders are rabbits, deer and voles, but squirrels and foxes can also wreak havoc in an ornamental or productive garden, especially in a rural setting. During spring, rabbits will frequently devour young and emerging perennial plants. Deer will eat stems, buds, leaves and bark of young trees, and voles cause damage in a similar way to deer, but much lower down, nearer to the ground. Tree guards, made from plastic and usually in green, brown or white, and metal tree protectors are useful for keeping the larger animals away. Special low vole guards are also available to stop these rodents.

Squirrels eat some fruits and dig up patches of lawn for places to bury nuts, or in search of previously buried ones. Unfortunately there aren't any proper squirrel controls for the amateur (foresters and farmers can trap them, shoot them and bait them with poison, but this is not practicable in a domestic garden). Also, as soon as you rid a family of squirrels from a garden, a new lot would move in.

Foxes don't cause too much trouble in the garden, although they can dig up and trample over plants. Dog foxes can create bad smells, and their urine can scorch conifers. As with squirrels, there is not a good, safe control for domestic situations. In gardens where foxes are a problem, the use of bonemeal or dried blood fertilizers should be avoided as the smell of them can make foxes think there is food present, and can result in more digging and foraging.

ABOVE **Wild rabbits can be real pests in a garden: they will eat soft plants, and they can strip young trees of their bark; damage is usually worst in the spring.**

OTHER NECESSARY PLANT MAINTENANCE

DEADHEADING

Loosely a form of pruning, deadheading is the removal of faded flowers before the plant has created the seed which follows. All cultivated flowering plants should be deadheaded. It saves the plant from wasting a huge amount of energy, and it can either encourage more flowers in the same year, or help to build up the plant for better flowering the following year.

Bedding plants and some soft perennials can be deadheaded and this may be best done with fingers, or a pair of shears (as you would, say, for lavender). Use a pair of secateurs to cut off the faded flowers on woody plants, cutting the stalks down as far as the first set of leaves.

ABOVE All flowering plants benefit from having their dead flowers removed. In some cases it just makes the plant look better, but in others – as with the roses seen here – it will encourage more flowers to be produced.

ABOVE Natural woody sticks and twigs can be pushed in and around perennial plants in spring to support them as they grow throughout spring and summer. In time the twigs will be completely obscured.

SUPPORTING CLIMBERS AND STAKING PERENNIALS

As new stems on climbing plants develop, they should be tied into wires or trelliswork, to avoid wind damage. Left untied they may break, or get in the way – and they would certainly spoil the overall appearance. Many medium and tall herbaceous plants (and annuals for that matter) will require some form of support to prevent them flopping over other plants, or in on themselves. Tie them to bamboo canes, or buy purpose-made wire hoop supports that are pushed in the ground for the plant to grow up and through.

These should be put in position in the early to mid-spring period, before the plants start growing apace.

ABOVE The modern alternative is purpose-made wire plant supports that are pushed in to the ground.

67

CHAPTER 6

Year-round care

The following pages serve as a reminder, an aide-mémoire, of some of the key jobs of which a gardener with an alkaline soil should be aware.

The gardening year is divided into 12; by all means think of them as 'months', but I am not going to label them 'January', 'February' and so on.

ABOVE Hardwood cuttings may be taken now of a wide range of ornamental and fruiting shrubs.

Depending on where you live, and from year-to-year, the weather for, say, October may be considerably warmer for you than another reader at the opposite end of the country. So it is far more appropriate to refer to the 12 divisions seasonally – and for you to decide, according to your location, which period is the most relevant for you.

EARLY WINTER

Digging: Now is the time to plan any changes to beds and borders. Areas to be planted with long-term shrubs and perennials should be dug over and plenty of organic matter incorporated into the top 18in (45cm) of soil. Allow the soil time to settle, before doing any planting.

Planting: New hardy shrubs may be planted on established ground (that is, ground that has been dug and given organic matter, ideally one to two months previously), on a day when the soil is not frozen or waterlogged. Before you dig the planting hole, give the area a final application of bonemeal fertilizer at 2oz per sq yd (65g per m^2), working this into the surface, treading the ground firm, and then raking it level.

Rhubarb: For an early crop of tender rhubarb, cover the dormant buds with straw or dry leaves inside a forcing pot or large bucket. All light should be excluded. The plant will produce tender stems in a few weeks' time.

Hardwood cuttings: Increase your stock of ornamental and fruiting shrubs at very little cost by taking hardwood cuttings. Select strong, healthy, ripened shoots of pencil thickness. Cut them into lengths of 6–9in (15–23cm). Trim the top with a slanting cut just above a bud, and the base with a square cut just below a bud. Remove leaves from the bottom two thirds of the cutting. Dip the base in fresh hormone rooting powder and push the cutting into a slit- or 'V'-shaped trench in the soil, made with a spade. Leave half to a third of the cutting visible above soil level. This is a good way to propagate alkaline-lovers such as golden bells (*Forsythia*), privet (*Ligustrum*), *Paulownia* and tamarisk (*Tamarix*).

ABOVE **Keep flowering displays in winter containers looking good by removing dead flowers and weeds.**

MID-WINTER

Slugs and snails: Take precautions now, before they start significant breeding. Use bait, beer traps or any other method except biological control, as it is too early in the gardening year, with the soil too cold, for this to work properly.

Tidy up winter containers: Baskets, window-boxes, beds and borders planted with winter- and spring-flowering plants should be looking good now. Keep displays at their best by regularly deadheading the flowers. Tidy up beds and borders, removing weeds as you go.

Shrubs in pots: Bring potted shrubs (which may include the acid lovers such as camellias, azaleas and rhododendrons that cannot grow in your alkaline garden soil) into a conservatory or cool, well-lit room, to force early flowers.

Prune roses: First, cut out dead, diseased and damaged wood, along with weak and spindly shoots. Then cut shoots of bush roses (hybrid teas and floribundas) to four to six buds from the base. Climbing roses may be pruned at this time; leave ramblers until late summer. Thriving plants will have produced a number of strong shoots during the previous summer, and the aim should be to keep five to seven of these and to tie them in well spaced apart. Remove as many as possible of the older flowered stems.

Prick over bulb beds: Spring bulbs, including tulips, daffodils and hyacinths, are appearing through the soil now. Go over the beds carefully with a small border fork, pricking the soil between the bulbs, but only to the depth of about 1in (2.5cm). This improves aeration, kills moss and loosens weeds for removal. Some varieties of bulbs may be in flower already; do not prick over these as you could damage them.

Planting: Hardy trees, shrubs, perennials and climbers may be planted on soil that was prepared a month or two previously.

MID-SPRING

Weeding not seeding: An old saying goes: 'One year's seeding leads to seven years' weeding'. It means that if you let your weeds grow and seed this year, you'll have to work hard over the next seven years to get rid of them! However, a bit of time spent hoeing on a dry day will soon clear away annual weed seedlings. Although this applies to every part of the garden, it is most important in the kitchen garden, as weeds growing between rows of vegetables are really difficult to control.

Stake border plants: By now perennial plants are producing an explosion of growth. The shoots that will eventually support the summer flowers are frequently quite brittle, which means that staking is needed. At first the stakes will be visible and seem to be obtrusive, but surrounding growth and the plant itself soon covers them. It is best to use natural twigs and sticks from other parts of the garden; these can be simply pushed in between the plants, and as long as they are firmly in place, and won't fall over in the slightest of breezes, they will do the job of supporting plants adequately. Modern manufactured stakes are good alternatives.

Trimming ivy: I do love to see houses covered in ivy, but it is not always good for the house. Ivy will work its way under roof tiles, into the eaves and into old mortar on houses that are already less than sound. You should be all right if your tiles are firmly in place and your brickwork is in good condition. Vigorous ivies will need to be trimmed several times throughout the growing season, and the first trim is usually around now.

Containers: Make up hanging baskets with a selection of bright bedding plants. Water them in, and keep the container in a greenhouse or sheltered place outside in readiness for hanging out when the weather warms up.

ABOVE **Many of the taller and 'floppier' perennial plants will need supporting, and this is a good time to put the supports in, before the shoots get too long.**

ABOVE **Hanging baskets can be planted up in mid-spring, but do not hang them out until all danger of frost is past.**

LATE SPRING

Taking cuttings: Propagating your favourite shrubs now is an absolute delight – the plant material is so fresh, firm and full of moisture that it can root very easily. And taking your own cuttings will save you money, too. Cuttings taken now will take up to three weeks before they have formed enough roots to pot up. The main danger during this time is that they will dry out – so keeping the compost moist and the atmosphere around the cuttings humid are top priorities. Take cuttings early in the morning or in the evening to avoid subjecting them to the heat of the day. Prepare 2–4in (5–10cm) long cuttings. Remove the lowest leaves, and leave two or three at the growing tip. Using a 3in (7.5cm) pot, insert each stem into cutting compost, so that the cuttings stand upright. Water it, then cover with a polythene bag. Suitable alkaline-loving shrubs for propagating now include: *Abelia, Ceratostigma, Forsythia, Lavandula, Lavatera, Philadelphus* and *Potentilla*.

Tulips: Lift tulips once leaves have faded. Dry out the bulbs by laying them in the sun before storing them in a dry, airy shed. Discard any damaged or diseased bulbs.

Tie-in climbers: As new stems on these plants develop, they should be tied in to their supports, to avoid wind damage. If this is done regularly, they should be in position to replace the older wood, which can be pruned out during the following mid-winter. Left untied they may well break, or at least be inflexible enough to make tying in later on more difficult.

Sowing vegetables: Leeks, sprouting broccoli, calabrese, cauliflowers, autumn cabbage and Brussels sprouts should be sown in a part of the vegetable garden. They will need to be transplanted into their final positions during the first half of the summer

ABOVE Take cuttings of favourite trees and shrubs in late spring, using soft new shoots.

ABOVE New shoots on climbing plants should be tied in to the supporting wires or trelliswork. This helps to create a more pleasing look, and prevents wind damage.

EARLY SUMMER

Feeding: Unless your soil is particularly fertile, established plants will benefit from another application of fertilizer. A balanced, general feed at the rate of 2oz per sq yd (65g per m²) will encourage blooms. Do not apply this feed beyond early summer, as it will promote growth of young stems that will not ripen before the onset of colder weather.

Hedges: Trim evergreen and conifer hedges now that nesting birds have moved on.

Thin fruit: Late frosts can occur, and these will reduce the amount of fruit set on trees. Where this happens the need for fruit thinning is reduced, but in other areas it is needed in order to get good-sized, high quality fruits. There is a natural drop of unwanted small fruits at this time but if, after this, there are still plenty of fruits, then thinning is necessary. Using your finger and thumb, start by removing any fruits that are damaged or badly shaped. Thin dessert apples and pears to leave one or two fruits per cluster, some 4in (10cm) apart or more; thin cooking apples so they are 6in (15cm) or more apart.

Pests and diseases: Aphids will be troublesome around now. The larvae of various caterpillars eat leaf, stem and flower tissue, reducing them to skeletons. Red spider mite can infect fruit trees as this time. For all these pests you should spray now. Also, spray the top and undersides of leaves with a fungicide as a precaution against mildew. Once the white mildew appears, spraying is ineffective.

Watering: Water plants as necessary, but pay particular attention to perennials and woody plants that were planted this spring. The first year of any new plant's life is the most vulnerable to 'drying out'.

ABOVE Once the white coating of mildew appears on leaves (here on a rose), spraying is ineffective.

LEFT Trim evergreen and conifer hedges in early summer, when there is reduced likelihood of nesting birds being present.

MID-SUMMER

Filling gaps in borders: If you have some unwanted gaps in beds and borders, there is still time to buy some colour to put in place for late summer and autumn. Look for trays or pots of *Nasturtium* (which thrives in dry, poor soil, and in containers); it will scramble quickly and effectively over fences and pergolas, too. Alkaline-loving annuals such as *Lavatera*, *Helianthus* and *Mimulus* will all look good until early autumn.

Prune flowering shrubs: Any shrubs that flowered during mid- to late spring can be pruned now, but remember: pruning is always necessary.

Sow biennials: Seed of forget-me-nots, wallflowers, Canterbury bells, sweet williams, double daisies and other spring-blooming biennials can be sown now in a quiet, semi-shaded part of the garden. Move them to their flowering positions in early autumn.

Grow your own mint collection: This is a good time to pot up some alkaline-loving mint. Mints, of which there are dozens of forms, vary hugely in both appearance and fragrance.

In the picture below there is the variegated applemint (*Mentha spicata* 'Variegata') in the front of the pot, with the taller and larger-leaved green Bowles' mint (*M.* x *villosa* 'Alopecuroides') behind. Flanked on either side is the reddish-tinged red paripila spearmint (*M. raripila rubra*). The first has a distinctly apple-and-mint flavour, and lasts longer into winter than most other mints. The Bowles' mint carries pink flowers, and the reddish mint has a sweet flavour and purple flowers in late summer. As if the flavour and appearance of mints are not enough, grow them for their pest control, as they can be used to deter aphids.

Watering: Continue to water plants as necessary. Water containers (tubs, windowboxes and hanging baskets) two or three times a week, even after heavy showers, which seldom soak the compost. Check them daily if they are in full sun for much of the day.

ABOVE All planted containers, including hanging baskets, dry out quickly in warm weather.

ABOVE Species of mint (*Mentha*) really need to be grown in containers otherwise they have the tendency to spread their roots all over the garden.

ABOVE Late summer is the time to prune rambler roses. Use sharp secateurs — and a pair of stout gloves.

ABOVE This is the start of the bulb planting season, so place your order now with specialist mail order suppliers, or buy your stocks from the garden centre.

LATE SUMMER

Sow late vegetables and herbs: Lettuces, radishes and endive can all be sown this late in the season. These will provide seedlings, some of which can be moved to a frame where they'll grow on with a bit of protection, while the others can be left to pick as and when necessary. A small sowing of stump-rooted carrots made now in a warm, sheltered part of the garden will continue the supply of young roots well into the autumn. Chives and parsley may also be sown: grow the seeds on, following the instructions on the packet, and the young, potted plants should be ready for planting out in spring next year.

Save seed: Select a few perennials or annuals and save the seed from them. If kept dry (in a sealed container) and frost-free over the winter period, the seed can be sown in late spring or early summer next year for a new crop of plants. Cut the seedheads off, while they are still green, and while the seedpods are swollen but before they are split. Place them in a container in a warm, dry place until the seedpods have ripened and spilled the contents. Remove any loose material from around the seeds, and store them until spring.

Order bulbs: Around now the specialist bulb nurseries are bringing out their mail-order catalogues for the forthcoming year. Choose your plants and place your orders early, particularly if you are wanting newly launched varieties, as stocks may run out.

Prune rambler roses: Late summer and into early autumn is the best time for pruning ramblers growing on sunless walls and fences. First untie all the stems from the supports so that you can see what's what.

Trim hedges: Continue to trim evergreen hedges and topiary specimens as necessary to keep them neat and tidy.

EARLY AUTUMN

Making compost: The compost heap is building up now that many herbaceous plants are being trimmed back to stop them sprawling. Make sure the layers in the heap are not too thick (in other words, do not put too much of any single thing – such as grass clippings – into the heap in one go). If you do it will turn to a stinking mush before it rots. It is a good idea to water each layer, to help the decomposing process. Also, cover the heap. If you have a compost bin it will already have a lid, which you should keep in place. If you have an open 'pen' affair, you should really cover the compost layer each time you add something, and a piece of old carpet is ideal.

Perennial borders: Tidy these by removing any supporting canes and storing them under cover. Cut back dead stems close to the crown. Weed the soil, and fork in natural fish, blood and bone meal to boost growth next spring.

Clearing early leaves: It may not be autumn proper yet, but it is not far away, and leaves are already beginning to fall. These are mainly from the deciduous shrubs that are not particularly known for their brilliant autumn tints. Don't let fallen leaves languish in borders (particularly on rockeries, where the little alpine plants can quickly succumb when smothered by soggy leaves), or in guttering.

Bulbs: Plant spring-flowering narcissi, tulips, hyacinths and others.

Feed lawns: Grass that is pale, hungry or otherwise less than perfect, should be given a feed now. Use a proprietary lawn fertilizer formulated for autumn use. Before you do this, however, it makes sense to put down a mosskiller to eradicate this problem if it is present. Mosskiller products are widely available.

ABOVE **Fallen leaves should not be allowed to remain on the ground as they can become slippery and dangerous, and they can kill patches of grass and smother delicate rockery plants.**

ABOVE **Compost heaps should be building up during spring, summer and autumn, but from early autumn it is a good idea to cover them up, to retain warmth within the heap.**

MID-AUTUMN

Autumn leaves: Remove dead leaves from flowerbeds, rockeries, lawns and footpaths. If left to rot in place they will harm, or even kill, the growing plants or grass beneath them. On paths they can become slippery and dangerous. Turn the leaves into leafmould. This is one of the most valuable of all garden by-products. Make a 'leaf pen' by choosing an out-of-the-way corner of the garden, knocking four posts into the ground in a square, and stretching wire netting around them. Fill the pen with fallen leaves, and put an old piece of carpet over the top to stop them blowing away. They take about a year to rot sufficiently for you to use the mixture as a mulch, or to dig in the soil.

Containers: Make up a few windowboxes, hanging baskets and tubs of seasonal winter flowers. Garden centres sell all of the component plants, and making up a container to your own design can be great fun. A small golden conifer (any kind will do, as long as it is small), with a trailing ivy and some silver foliage (*Senecio maritima*) can look great all winter. The bonus is that all of these can be planted out in the garden in spring. Keep the compost on the dry side, and make sure the pots have good drainage.

Autumn tidy-up: After the larger perennials have finished their display, remove the supports. Clean, dry and store them. If you used twiggy sticks, you should burn or dispose of them, because they can harbour pests and diseases.

Hedges: Trim hornbeam, beech and other deciduous hedges; keep the base wide and taper in towards the top.

Peas and beans: Traditionally, this is the time to make a winter sowing of peas. Use the hardy, round-seed cultivars such as 'Feltham First', 'Douce Provence' or 'Oregon Sugarpod'. Hardy broad beans may also be sown now.

ABOVE Mid-autumn is a good time to plant up containers with plants that will give winter interest and colour.

ABOVE A sowing of winter-hardy, round-seeded peas may be made in mid-autumn; choose carefully which variety you sow now as not all peas will endure winter outdoors.

LATE AUTUMN

Tidy up borders: By this time most herbaceous plants will have lost most of their leaves and many will have died down to practically nothing. Cut off all remaining dead and dying stems and leaves (but make sure you leave the green leaves and stems of *Helleborus*).

Spring bedding: It is getting to the stage now when spring bedding should be in. Once the summer bedding has been cleared, lightly fork over the soil, removing any weeds, and then rake it level. Pot-grown and tray bedding plants should be watered a couple of hours prior to planting. Start at the back of the border with taller plants, such as wallflowers, following through to shorter-growing edging plants such as double daisies, violas and primroses. Space wallflowers, primulas and polyanthus 12in (30cm) apart, sweet williams, pansies and violas 9–12in (23–30cm) apart and forget-me-nots 6–9in (15–23cm) apart.

Make sure all the plants are firmed in well (frosts can 'lift' the plants and expose the delicate roots).

Asparagus: If you grow this delicious alkaline-loving vegetable, over the coming weeks you will have to cut back its fern-like foliage. It should not be cut back before it turns yellow, as this will weaken the plant. Cut it back to 2–3in (5–7cm) above soil level.

Service tools: If secateurs and pruners are not cutting cleanly, sharpen the angled side of the blade on a fine carborundum or oil stone. The same abrasive surface will do for sharpening pruning or cutting knives. Afterwards, smear the blades with an oily rag, and put a drop of oil on pivots. Scrape and wash clean other tools, and wipe metal parts with an oily rag, and wooden parts with a linseed oil-covered rag.

Pruning: This is generally a good time to carry out major pruning of large tree branches – as long as the weather is not wet or frosty.

ABOVE The best time to give all of your hand tools a good clean and a 'service' is at the end of the season. Scrape off mud, scrub them clean and then wipe an oily rag over them to prevent rust.

ABOVE Bedding plants should be planted now, to provide colour in spring. These wallflowers should be spaced 12in (30cm) apart.

**TYPICAL PLANT
HARDINESS ZONES FOR
WESTERN EUROPE**

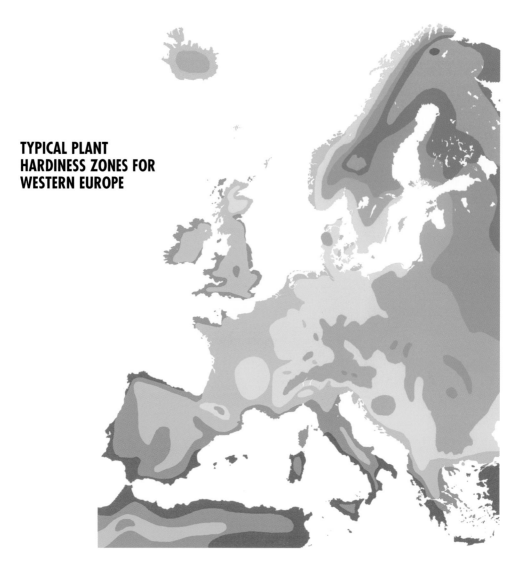

Gardening on chalk and limestone can be frustrating. There are limitations as to what one can do and grow, and the aim of this book is to show the ways of overcoming or working a way around these limitations.

Another concern, however, is the climate. There are chalk landscapes right across the planet, and this means that there are indigenous, alkaline-loving plants growing in practically all climate zones.

By reading these pages you can determine which plants are right for your soil, but how can you tell if they are suited also to your climate?

Of course, new plants are being developed all the time, and often hardiness and other weather tolerances, that are bred into them. So, when buying plants, it is useful to know which sort of climate best suits them – the areas of the world in which they originated usually dictate this.

If you live in Europe or the US, the maps on these pages will give you an indication of the plant hardiness zones for your area.

The Directory shows that plants for alkaline soils can be adaptable, so wherever you live you should be able to find good plants that suit you and your garden's requirements.

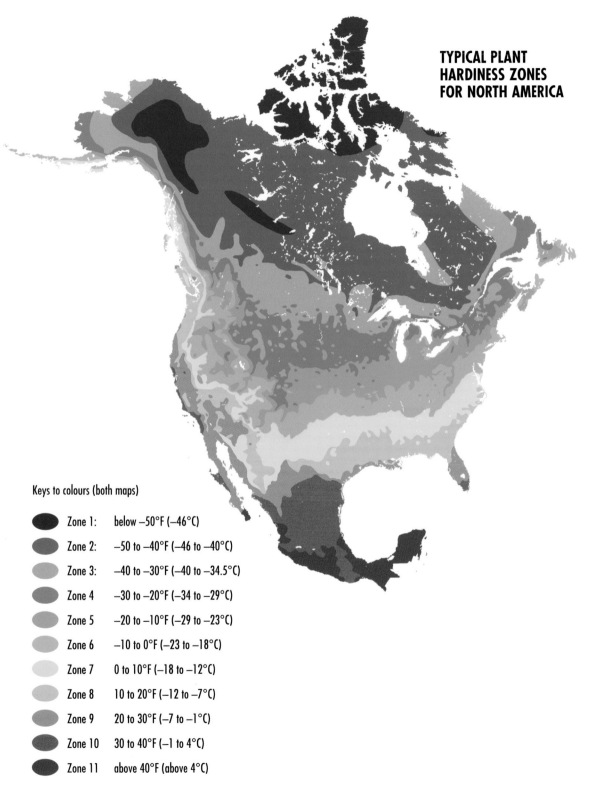

TYPICAL PLANT HARDINESS ZONES FOR NORTH AMERICA

Keys to colours (both maps)

Zone 1:   below −50°F (−46°C)

Zone 2:   −50 to −40°F (−46 to −40°C)

Zone 3:   −40 to −30°F (−40 to −34.5°C)

Zone 4   −30 to −20°F (−34 to −29°C)

Zone 5   −20 to −10°F (−29 to −23°C)

Zone 6   −10 to 0°F (−23 to −18°C)

Zone 7   0 to 10°F (−18 to −12°C)

Zone 8   10 to 20°F (−12 to −7°C)

Zone 9   20 to 30°F (−7 to −1°C)

Zone 10   30 to 40°F (−1 to 4°C)

Zone 11   above 40°F (above 4°C)

CHAPTER 7

A–Z plant directory

This part of the book will be an invaluable source of reference when you are choosing plants for your alkaline soil. Listed here are many of our most popular garden plants for such situations; they are listed alphabetically – by Latin name – within the section that relates to their type (annuals, bulbs, perennials, trees and shrubs and so on).

Under each of the descriptions are these items of information:

Origin: This tells you, if known, where the species was discovered. Understanding where a plant comes from, the country or part of the world, with its average climate or even altitude, can help you to understand its growing requirements and conditions.

Type: The 'type' of plant – for example, whether it is grown from a bulb as opposed to a tuber, corm or rhizome, or whether it is an annual (grows, flowers and dies within one year) or a biennial (the same but in two years), or perhaps a shrub rather than a climber.

USDA zone: These are the climate zones referred to on pages 82 and 83, designed to identify the relative hardiness of plants. The zone numbers quoted here, based on UK Royal Horticultural Society data, are on the cautious side, so if you are not prepared to take any

chances, follow the hardiness ratings to the letter. Otherwise there is a great deal of leeway. Raised beds, good drainage, tree cover, east-facing as opposed to west-facing gardens, and planting against a house wall all give plants a better habitat – so be prepared to experiment.

Preferred pH range: The plants included in this Directory are likely to thrive if the soil in which they are growing is between the range of pH points given. This is the optimum acidity level for the particular plant in question. However, if your soil is higher or lower than the pH range in question it does not necessarily mean that your plants will die, nor that the situation is impossible to rectify. The pH can be made higher or lower accordingly, by following the processes discussed on pages 21–25.

Description: Here you will discover generalized details of the plant's shape, size and general demeanour, along with flower and foliage colour and shape.

Popular species and varieties: Sometimes a plant species will exist without offspring or siblings. This will therefore have a relatively small entry in this book. But with, for example, the *Papaver* (poppy) genus, there are dozens of different species and *cultivars* (abbreviation of 'cultivated variety'), so there will be many to recommend.

Award of Garden Merit

Throughout this A–Z Directory you will see the initials AGM set after certain plants. This denotes that the plant in question has passed certain assessments carried out by experts under the auspices of the Royal Horticultural Society in Great Britain. Only plants with exceptionally good garden qualities – such as colour, habit, form and length of flowering period – can be awarded this special Award of Garden Merit.

ANNUALS AND BIENNIALS

NAME: *BRACHYCOME IBERIDIFOLIA* (SWAN RIVER DAISY)

Origin: South Australia
Type: Half-hardy annual
USDA Zone: Z8 (only relevant if sown in the autumn for overwintering outside)
Preferred pH range: 6.5–8.0
Description: This gorgeous, free-flowering daisy plant blooms right through summer and well into autumn, in fact until the first frosts cause the plant to decline quickly. It is one of the easiest plants to grow, and is good for amateurs and beginners, as it rarely fails to delight. It thrives in a dry and sunny position, and is most attractive in the front of mixed flower borders and amongst roses.

Plants reach a height of 12in (30cm). Sow seed under glass in spring and plant out after the frosts, some 6–9in (15–23cm) apart, or sow later outside in its flowering position, and thin out the seedlings.

Popular species and varieties: 'White Splendour' is crisp white, and perfect as an accent plant in a border, or to cool down hot colours of surrounding plants. 'Purple Splendour' produces masses of purple-blue heads, and 'Summer Skies' is a mix of sweetly scented pretty pastel shades. 'Dwarf Bravo Mixed' is a superb cushion-forming, compact mix of dark and light blue, violet and white, each flower with either a black or yellow centre.

ABOVE *Brachycome* 'Purple Splendour'

NAME: *CONVOLVULUS TRICOLOR* (DWARF MORNING GLORY)

Origin: Portugal, Greece and North Africa

Type: Short-lived perennial, usually grown as a hardy annual

USDA Zone: Z8 (only relevant if sown in the autumn for overwintering outside)

Preferred pH range: 6.0–8.0

Description: This relative of the pernicious bindweed, but which has none of its evil characteristics, flowers freely in summer and autumn. It thrives in a light soil in a sunny spot. Sow seed in its flowering season in spring and thin out to 12in (30cm) apart. It looks superb massed in beds and, due to its semi-trailing habit, can also be grown in hanging baskets.

Popular species and varieties: Flags seem to be a theme with cultivar names of *Convolvulus*, because of the bright colours enjoyed by both. 'Flagship Mixed' is a superior mix of bright colours, including light and dark blue, pink and red, but each flower has a strikingly coloured centre. 'Red Ensign' and 'Blue Ensign' are colours from this mix that are available separately, each flower having the main colour but with white and yellow centres.

NAME: *COSMOS BIPINNATUS*

Origin: Central America, Mexico

Type: Half-hardy annual

USDA Zone: Z8/9 (only relevant if sown in the autumn for overwintering outside)

Preferred pH range: 6.0–8.0

Description: This annual is excellent both as a garden plant and when grown for cutting and bringing indoors for arrangements. It is a showy plant with flowers appearing throughout summer and early autumn. Plant it at the mid-point or back of the border, or in large massed plantings. Plants can grow up to 8ft (2.5m), but usually reach 3–4ft (1–1.2m). The habit is open, and branching, and the foliage is bright green and lacy. The daisy-like flowers are 3–6in (7.5–15cm) wide, and are single, double, or crested. They have white, pink, crimson or lavender petals, often notched or frilled, with yellow centres.

Popular species and varieties: 'Sensation Mixed' comprises a large selection of shades in whites, pinks and carmine-reds. 'Candy Stripe' has ice-white blooms, boldly bordered, splashed or stippled with crimson (occasionally a pure crimson bloom may appear); 'Daydream' has smaller flowers than most, and they are freely produced; and 'Pied Piper Red' has fluted shell-like petals of velvet crimson-red.

ABOVE *Convolvulus* '**Flagship Mixed**'

ABOVE *Cosmos* '**Sensation Pink**'

NAME: *DIANTHUS BARBATUS* (SWEET WILLIAM)

Origin: Throughout Europe, Asia and the eastern US
Type: Biennial
USDA Zone: Z5–8
Preferred pH range: 6.5–8.5
Description: The sweet william is a wonderfully familiar kind of plant, many of us having seen it in the gardens of our grandparents, for 50 years ago it was much more popular is it is today. As well as a good plant for bulking out flowerbeds in summer, sweet williams are also excellent as cut flowers, and fillers in immature beds and borders. Compact varieties make a cheerful edging to rock gardens. Reaching 1–2ft (30–60cm) in height, the flowers are numerous in red, rose-purple, white, or variously coloured. Sometimes the blooms are double, and they are nearly always spicily fragrant.
Popular species and varieties: There are a great number of varieties (and mixtures) to choose and grow from seed. They include: 'Noverna' (in shades of red, pink and purple), 'Excelsior Mixed' (strongly scented); 'Indian Carpet Mixed' and 'Nanus' (just 6in [15cm] high) and 'Roundabout' (red-centred flowers of magenta, rose-pink, carmine and white).

NAME: *ESCHSCHOLZIA* CALIFORNICA AGM (CALIFORNIAN POPPY)

Origin: California to Oregon
Type: Hardy annual
USDA Zone: Z6
Preferred pH range: 6.5–8.0
Description: This is the state flower of California, and flowers throughout summer. The silky-textured poppy-like blooms look attractive among annuals, perennials and in rock gardens. Sow seed in its flowering position in spring and thin out seedlings to 12in (30cm) apart. It can also be sown in autumn in milder climates for earlier flowering the following year. Available in mixtures or separate colours.
Popular species and varieties: 'Strawberry Fields' is not so much strawberry-red as tangerine-orange, but for all this it is a superb plant adding richness of colour to a border. 'Milkmaid' has deep cream fluted blooms above ferny blue-green foliage; 'Golden Values' is a lovely, warm yellow with rich, golden orange centres; 'Ivory Castle' has creamy-white flowers with pretty yellow stamens and feathery foliage; and 'Rose Chiffon' has silky, double blooms of pinky rose with contrasting golden yellow centres.

ABOVE *Dianthus barbatus* 'Noverna Purple'

ABOVE *Eschscholzia california* 'Strawberry Fields'

NAME: *HELIOTROPIUM ARBORESCENS* (HELIOTROPE, or CHERRY PIE)

Origin: Tropical and temperate regions throughout the world

Type: Half-hardy perennial usually treated as an annual

USDA Zone: Z10

Preferred pH range: 7.0–8.0

Description: Cultivars of this half-hardy deciduous perennial (which, in frost-prone climates, is generally grown as an annual summer bedding or pot plant) have purple, violet-blue or white flowers. The blooms, which really do smell of fresh cherry pie, appear continuously throughout summer and early autumn. Heliotrope can be used effectively as 'dot' plants in summer bedding schemes, combining well with pelargoniums, begonias, impatiens, petunias and marigolds. Sow seeds in spring, or take cuttings in late summer, overwintering the plants in a cool, frost-free greenhouse.

Popular species and varieties: *Heliotropium arborescens* is the species from which most of the summer cultivars arise. Look for 'Marine' (wine purple), 'Nagano' (deep lavender) and 'P.K. Lowther' (pale purple).

ABOVE *Heliotropium* 'P.K. Lowther'

NAME: *LAVATERA TRIMESTRIS* (MALLOW)

Origin: Mediterranean

Type: Hardy annual

USDA Zone: Z7 (only relevant if sown in the autumn for overwintering outside)

Preferred pH range: 6.5–8.0

Description: One of the easiest of annuals to grow, it flowers profusely all through the summer. It is useful for cutting and for filling empty spaces in mixed borders. Sow seed in its flowering position in the spring and thin out seedlings to 18–24in (45–60cm) apart.

Popular species and varieties: 'Mont Blanc' is covered in large, blousy blooms of crisp, linen white; it is one of the fastest-growing annuals, creating a shrub-sized bush in less than 12 weeks. 'Silver Cup' is an award-winning variety with bright pink trumpet flowers, each petal with darker pink veining; and 'Ruby Regis' has masses of veined, deep carmine blooms.

ABOVE *Lavatera* 'Mont Blanc'

NAME: *LIMNANTHES DOUGLASII* AGM (POACHED EGG FLOWER)

Origin: Coastal western US
Type: Hardy annual
USDA Zone: Z8
Preferred pH range: 6.5–8.0
Description: This is given its common name because the blooms have yellow centres and are surrounded by white. Each flower is saucer-shaped, and the blooms are produced on 6in (15cm) high stems, accompanied by deeply cut light green leaves. The blooms open in early summer, and are 1in (2.5cm) or so across. Bees have a particular liking for the flowers of *Limnanthes*, which are delicately scented. Sow seed outside in spring, where the plants are to flower. In milder gardens, autumn-sown seed can flower earlier than spring-sown seed and, if you have a greenhouse or conservatory, seed sown in pots in early autumn can flower throughout winter and spring.
Popular species and varieties: Usually just the straight species is seen.

ABOVE *Limnanthes douglasii* AGM

NAME: *MIMULUS* (MONKEY FLOWER)

Origin: North and South America
Type: Perennial, but treated as an annual
USDA Zone: Typically Z7–10
Preferred pH range: 6.0–8.0
Description: As much as these plants like an alkaline soil, it is even more important for them to have a moist soil. In fact, they'll usually quite happily survive in the shallows of a pond edge. The parent species grows in Chilean bogs, and the hybrids retain a trace of this characteristic. They are versatile enough to be successfully grown in windowboxes or small gardens in part shade. Forms of *Mimulus* are rather short-lived and make a bright show of colour in summer with their tubular blooms of velvety petals spotted at the flower throat. They come in a range of reds, oranges, yellows and bicolours.
Popular species and varieties: The hybrids 'Big Boy' and 'Magic Series' both have large and vividly coloured blooms. *Mimulus cupreus* has bronzy-orange, brown-spotted flowers, with a height and spread of 12in (30cm). *M. cardinalis* (red and yellow flowers) grows to a height of 24in (60cm) and a spread of 12in (30cm); *M. luteus* (yellow, crimson-spotted) has a variable height from 6–24in (16–60cm) and a spread of some 12in (30cm).

ABOVE *Mimulus* 'Magic Series'

NAME: *MOLUCELLA LAEVIS* (BELLS OF IRELAND)

Origin: Western Asia
Type: Half-hardy annual
USDA Zone: Z7
Preferred pH range: 6.5–8.0
Description: This plant has somewhat inconspicuous flowers, each surrounded by a large, light green calyx. When the seeds form, these calyces become papery, and at this stage the seed heads are good for drying. *Molucella* is suitable for a sunny mixed border, and looks good planted with low-growing yellow annuals (such as marigolds), or blue annuals (such an *Nigella* or *Nemophila*). Sow the seeds in early to mid-spring in the greenhouse or frame, or outside in their flowering positions at the latter end of the season.
Popular species and varieties: Usually only the species is grown.

NAME: *PHLOX DRUMMONDII* (ANNUAL PHLOX)

Origin: US (Texas)
Type: Half-hardy annual
USDA Zone: Z6
Preferred pH range: 7.0–8.0
Description: These easy-to-grow half-hardy annuals will give a succession of colour throughout summer. In spring sow seeds under glass in a temperature of 16°C (60°F). The young plants should be ready for planting out in the garden once all frosts are past; set them at 9in (23cm) spacings.
Popular species and varieties: For a really bright summer display try *Phlox drummondii* 'Carnival' with pink, rose, salmon, scarlet, blue and violet flowers. These are carried on stems 12in (30cm) high, accompanied by light green foliage. 'Twinkle Stars' is a popular mix with magenta and white flowers.

ABOVE *Molucella laevis*

ABOVE *Phlox* 'Twinkle Stars'

ANNUALS AND BIENNIALS PREFERRING SOILS IN THE NEUTRAL RANGE

The following plants thrive in a soil with a pH range that straddles both the higher levels of acidity and the lower levels of alkalinity

Latin name	Common name	pH range
Ageratum	Floss flower	6.0–7.5
Althaea	Hollyhock	6.0–7.5
Alyssum	Madwort/Alyssum	6.0–7.5
Anchusa	Bugloss/Alkanet	6.0–7.5
Armeria	Thrift	6.0–7.5
Aster	Starwort/Daisy plant/Michaelmas daisy	5.5–7.5
Calceolaria	Slipper flower	6.0–7.5
Campanula	Canterbury bells	6.0–7.5
Centaurea	Cornflower/Knapweed	5.5–7.5
Dianthus	Annual carnation/Sweet william	6.5–8.5
Digitalis	Foxglove	6.0–7.5
Erysimum	Wallflower	5.5–7.5
Gaillardia	Blanket flower	6.0–7.5
Godetia	Farewell-to-spring	6.0–7.5
Gypsophila	Baby's breath	6.0–7.5
Helianthus	Sunflower	6.0–7.5
Iberis	Candytuft	6.0–7.5
Ipomoea	Morning glory	6.0–7.5
Lobelia	Lobelia	6.0–7.5
Leucanthemum	Marguerite	6.0–7.5
Lathyrus	Sweet pea	6.0–7.5
Matthiola	Stock	6.0–7.5
Nasturtium	Nasturtium	5.5–7.5
Papaver	Poppy	6.0–7.5
Petunia	Petunia	6.0–7.5
Portulaca	Sun plant/Ross moss	5.5–8.0
Pyrethrum	Pyrethrum	6.0–7.5
Salvia	Salvia/Sage	6.0–7.5
Scabiosa	Scabious	5.0–8.0
Zinnia	Zinnia/Youth-and-old-age	5.5–8.0

ABOVE *Allium christophii* AGM

ABOVE *Allium flavum*

BULBS

ALLIUM (ORNAMENTAL ONION)

Origin: Throughout the Northern Hemisphere
Type: Bulbous perennials
USDA Zone: Z5–9
Preferred pH range: 6.0–8.5
Description: Onions growing in the vegetable garden are one thing, but ornamental species in the flower garden are something entirely different. Both are essential in their appropriate places. The decorative alliums are grown for their round flowerheads comprising masses of short, tubular flowers. They are generally in shades of blue, purple, pink or white, but there are also a few outstanding yellow species. Alliums have long leaves, either thick or strap-shaped. Sometimes these leaves die down before the flowers appear. Grow them in a mixed border, where they associate well with most broad-leaved perennials and low-growing shrubs.

Popular species and varieties: One of the most popular is *Allium christophii* AGM, sometimes referred to as the Star of Persia. It grows to 18in (45cm) in height, and has strap-shaped grey-green leaves The large rounded flowerhead, which can be 6in (15cm) or more across, consists of many small star-shaped silvery pink blooms, in late spring. *A. giganteum* AGM, an expensive monster, produces large, purple globe flowers on stems 5ft (1.5m) high in mid-summer. *A. caeruleum* AGM has bright blue star-shaped flowers in early summer. *A. sphaerocephalon* produces egg-shaped flowerheads of salmon pink and brick-red. Of the yellow species, look for *A. moly* (known as golden garlic), with its golden yellow flowers, spreading rapidly, and *A. flavum*, which has bright yellow flowers so arranged in the head that they give a Roman candle effect.

ABOVE *Allium giganteum* AGM

ARUM ITALICUM (LORDS AND LADIES)

Origin: Throughout Europe and Asia
Type: Tuberous perennials
USDA Zone: Z6–7
Preferred pH range: 6.5–8.0
Description: This plant is particularly useful for a woodland garden, producing much needed fresh and bright foliage in the depths of winter. Its marbled leaves are often used by flower arrangers, as indeed are the fruiting spikes comprising thick clusters of bright orange-red berries. Attractive though they are, the berries are poisonous. The flowers are typical of the *Arum* family in that they comprise a flat, spade-like structure, called a 'spathe'.

The *Arum* genus should not be confused with the large summer-flowering *Zantedeschia aethiopeca* (see page 102), with dramatic white spathes, which is known as the arum lily.

Popular species and varieties: *Arum italicum* subsp. *italicum* 'Marmoratum' is the best form; it used to be referred to simply as 'Pictum'. The hybrid 'Chameleon' produces large, more rounded leaves with greyish markings on them, whilst 'White Winter' should be grown for its dramatic silver foliage. *A. concinnatum* produces a flower of dull yellow, or often creamy purple, whilst the yellow-spathed *A. creticum* can sometimes be found in other colour forms.

ABOVE *Arum italicum*

NAME: *CAMASSIA* (QUAMASH)

Origin: North and South America
Type: Bulbous perennials
USDA Zone: Z3–7
Preferred pH range: 6.5–8.0
Description: These plants are among the few bulbs that prefer a heavy damp soil. They are excellent in a mixed border, combining well with late spring- or early summer-flowering shrubs. The fairly large flowers are generally star-shaped, in shades of blue or white, and carried on tall stems. The long narrow, upright leaves are bright green. Once planted, leave the plants undisturbed for several years to steadily build them up into sizeable clumps. In areas with hard winters the plants benefit from a permanent mulch of organic matter to protect the bulbs from frost. The flowers are suitable for cutting and bringing inside for arrangements. The best impact in the garden is where a dozen or so bulbs are grown in a group.

Popular species and varieties: *Camassia cusickii* grows to 20in (50cm) in height, and its silvery-blue flowers are suspended over a rosette of broad greyish foliage. *C. cusickii* 'Zwanenburg' has deep purple-blue flowers. *C. quamash* (sometimes listed as *C. esculenta*) grows to around 24in (60cm); the flowers range in colour from blue and purple to white. *C. leichtlinii* subsp. *leichtlinii* (also sometimes found as 'Alba') produces attractive white flowers. *C. leichtlinii* Caerulea Group has deep mauve-blue flowers. *C. leichtlinii* subsp. *suksdorfii* is a reliable plant with 36in (90cm) high flowering stems, with blue flowers.

ABOVE *Camassia cusickii* 'Zwanenburg'

ABOVE *Crocosmia* 'Firebird'

ABOVE *Crocosmia* 'Star of the East' AGM

CROCOSMIA (MONTBRETIA)

Origin: South Africa
Type: Perennial corm
USDA Zone: Z7
Preferred pH range: 6.5–8.0
Description: These hardy herbaceous perennials grow from corms, and are valued for their brilliantly coloured, somewhat funnel-shaped flowers. In mid-summer few can fail to notice a well-established group of bright red montbretia in all its glory. They produce clumps of upright, sword-shaped, or grassy leaves.

Popular species and varieties: *Crocosmia masoniorum* AGM has typical slightly arching foliage. Its red-orange flowers are held on stems 5ft (1.5m) in height. Individual blooms comprise long tubes, with well spread petals and prominent stamens. When it comes to the named varieties there is certainly plenty of choice. There is a considerable number of yellow forms, including 'Citronella', and the later-flowering 'Solfatare' AGM, its blooms an attractive apricot-yellow over bronze-flushed foliage. There is the fiery-red 'Vulcan', and the very popular 'Lucifer' AGM, another brilliant red. 'Firebird' has orange-red flowers. 'Jackanapes' is a shorter plant than most, with masses of smallish flowers that are orange on the outside and yellow on the inside. 'Star of the East' AGM is one of the most spectacular forms, with golden-orange flowers with a yellow eye opening from orange-red buds. It was bred by George Davison, a famous breeder in the mid-twentieth century; after developing this plant he turned his attention to breeding apples, in the belief that 'Star of the East' could never be surpassed.

NAME: *CROCUS*

Origin: Mid- and Southern Europe, Middle East, Central Asia and Northern Africa
Type: Perennial corm
USDA Zone: Z4–8
Preferred pH range: 6.0–8.0
Description: Who can fail to enjoy the sight of crocuses in late winter and early spring? Most are easy to grow, free-flowering and increase well in suitable conditions. There are over 80 species, native to parts of the world as diverse as the Mediterranean at one extreme, and high alpine regions at the other. Despite flowering early, weak sunshine in mild weather will encourage them to open their flowers wide, making a splendid show particularly when naturalized. They die back quickly after flowering so it is not usually necessary to restrict grass cutting. Whilst many of the species can be grown in our gardens, those most likely to be found are cultivars.

Popular species and varieties: Dutch crocuses are the most widely grown of all. There is a fine range of cultivars available, and most are robust, free-flowering plants with larger blooms than the species. Flowering later than their smaller cousins they also increase rapidly. Often sold as mixed colours, one should not overlook the potential of growing smaller groups of the same variety. Look out for the pure white 'Jeanne d'Arc', the rich purple-violet 'Queen of the Blues', the silvery lilac-blue 'Vanguard', and 'Pickwick' with its striking purple-striped blooms. *Crocus tommasinianus* AGM is one of the first to flower, in late winter and early spring. Its soft lavender flowers are small and slender. There are a number of varieties. Look for: 'Whitwell Purple'(purplish-blue) and 'Ruby Giant' (deep purple). Crocuses in the Chrysanthus group are free-flowering. Growing to around 3in (7cm) in height, they are at their best from late winter to early spring, depending on conditions. Highly recommended are 'Cream Beauty' AGM (a lovely soft cream-yellow), 'Snow Bunting' AGM (white), 'Blue Pearl' AGM (a delicate blue with a bronze base and silvery blue on the outside of the petals) and 'Advance' (a deep all-over golden yellow). A few species of *Crocus* also flower in the autumn: the saffron crocus, *C. sativus* (large purple flowers with three deep red stigmas that are the source of the spice saffron); and *C. kotschyanus* AGM (pale lilac yellow-throated blooms).

ABOVE *Crocus tommasinianus* 'Whitwell Purple'

ABOVE *Crocus chrysanthus* 'Advance'

ABOVE *Eranthis hyemalis* Tubergenii Group 'Guinea Gold' AGM

ERANTHIS HYEMALIS (WINTER ACONITE)

Origin: Southern Europe
Type: Rhizomatous perennial
USDA Zone: Z5
Preferred pH range: 6.0–8.0
Description: The buttercup-yellow, cup-shaped blooms of *Eranthis* are a really cheery sight in late winter. The flowers, supported by collars of green, deeply toothed bracts, distinguish these from other winter plants such as hellebores and snowdrops; they are like nothing else, and every garden should try to make room for one or two of them.
Popular species and varieties: The common winter aconite (*Eranthis hyemalis* AGM) will grow anywhere, even under beech trees. It will seed itself if the conditions are right, and will in time form a large carpet of late-winter colour. *E. hyemalis* Tubergenii Group has larger blooms, and the form 'Guinea Gold' AGM is particularly vigorous. Both of these never become a nuisance, making compact little clumps with rich yellow flowers in early spring.

NAME: *EUCOMIS* (PINEAPPLE LILY)

Origin: Sub-tropical Africa
Type: Bulbous perennial
USDA Zone: Z8
Preferred pH range: 6.0–8.0
Description: This is sometimes treated as a greenhouse plant, but in mild areas it can grow outside perfectly well, if it has a very sheltered position at the base of a sunny wall. It takes its common name from its flower spike, which resembles that of a pineapple with its top crown of tufted leaves. *Eucomis* is an excellent plant for containers on a sunny patio.
Popular species and varieties: The species most commonly seen is *Eucomis bicolor* AGM which grows to around 30in (75cm) in height, with its green and purple-edged flower spike about 12in (30cm) long. The stout stem is also heavily blotched with purple. There is also a white form listed as 'Alba'. *E. comosa* is green and brown. *E. regia* produces dense spikes of green and purple. Mid-summer onwards is when *E. autumnalis* produces its flowering spikes of pure white; attractive seedheads then follow.

ABOVE *Eucomis comosa*

NAME: *GALANTHUS* (SNOWDROP)

Origin: Western Europe
Type: Bulbous perennial
USDA Zone: Z4–6
Preferred pH range: 6.0–8.0
Description: To the untrained eye all snowdrops look very similar, with their nodding white flowers. They are one of our favourite winter-flowering bulbs. However, there are many species and cultivars, with many different, yet subtle markings, shades, shapes, sizes and so on. There is an almost cult following, with enthusiasts studying the minutia of flower differences. Nearly all are best in part shade, although *Galanthus elwesii* AGM is better in full sun. Garden snowdrops can frequently cross-pollinate, resulting in young plants (seedlings) springing up in different places, with slightly different flowers from the parents.

Popular species and varieties: The most widely grown species is that of the common snowdrop (*Galanthus nivalis* AGM). It grows from 4–8in (10–20cm) high, and produces its finest show in a fertile soil. The blue-grey leaves are flat and strap-shaped; the white flowers have small green markings on the central sets of petals. 'Flore Pleno' AGM is a double form, and among the named varieties look for 'S. Arnott' AGM, which is slightly scented, and 'Viridapicis' with a green spot on both the inner and outer petals. 'Lady Elphinstone' has yellow markings. *G. elwesii* AGM is often called the giant snowdrop. Its broad, grey-blue leaves accompany the large flowers on 10in (25cm) high stems. The blooms have three long petals, and three shorter ones with bright green markings.

ABOVE *Galanthus elwesii* AGM

IPHEION (SPRING STARFLOWER)

Origin: South America
Type: Bulbous perennial
USDA Zone: Z6
Preferred pH range: 6.5–8.0
Description: These delightful and easy-to-grow plants are perfect for sunny pockets on the rock garden, containers, or edging paths, and are very useful for naturalizing among other spring-flowering bulbs. This plant is a member of the onion family, and the leaves emit an onion smell when crushed.
Popular species and varieties: *Ipheion uniflorum* produces masses of narrow grey-green leaves in late winter. The slightly fragrant, pale blue star-shaped flowers are carried on 6in (15cm) high stems in early spring. Several varieties are available: 'Album' is pure white; 'Wisley Blue' AGM produces violet-blue flowers in late spring; and 'Froyle Mill' AGM is a slightly pinker shade. Best grown in a cool greenhouse or sunny, sheltered spot outside, the hybrid 'Rolf Fiedler' AGM is a lovely clear blue.

ABOVE *Oxalis adenophylla* AGM

OXALIS (SORREL or SHAMROCK)

Origin: South Africa and South America
Type: Tuberous perennials
USDA Zone: Z3–8
Preferred pH range: 6.5–8.0
Description: The *Oxalis* family is extremely large, with some 800 species, some of which are very invasive and are considered to be weeds in the worst sense. However there are some that make excellent garden plants. These tuberous perennials generally prefer a sunny position, and they nearly always have clover-like leaves. They are suitable for borders, rockeries and containers. I consider them to be among the most beautiful of spring flowers.
Popular species and varieties: *Oxalis adenophylla* AGM has a dwarf habit, growing to just 4in (10cm) in height, and is arguably best grown on a rock garden. In spring it produces a neat rosette of crinkled grey-green leaves, which are soon followed by the rose-pink and white flowers, held on strong stalks. *O. obtusa* produces tufts of trifoliate leaves and wide funnel-shaped blooms of a rich sugar pink. *O. depressa* is a free-flowering species with masses of bright rose-pink flowers over grey-green leaves. *O. lobata* produces tufts of bright green leaves in spring, and then they disappear. A new crop of leaves appear in the autumn, and this time they are accompanied by golden yellow flowers.

ABOVE *Ipheion uniflorum*

NAME: *SCILLA (SQUILL)*

Origin: USSR, Iran
Type: Bulbous perennials
USDA Zone: Z5–6
Preferred pH range: 6.5–8.0
Description: Between mid-winter and mid-spring these tough little plants can produce a veritable carpet of pale blue, dark blue and near white. They may be grown in a sunny spot, but they are best in a lightly shaded position at the edge of a border, or in the rock garden. They make good windowbox plants, too.
Popular species and varieties: The best-known family member, *Scilla sibirica* AGM, is the loveliest and easiest species. Its leaves make their appearance in early spring and are soon followed by the 4in (10cm) stems carrying three or four blue, bell-shaped flowers. *S. sibirica* 'Spring Beauty' is a robust form with larger bright blue flowers. 'Alba' is a good white-flowering variety. The dainty *S. bifolia* AGM produces two strap-shaped leaves which open out to allow a 4in (10cm) high stem, holding blue star-shaped flowers, in late winter. 'Rosea' is a purple-pink form and 'Alba' is white. *S. verna* has electric-blue flowers in spring. *S. mischtschenkoana* has pale blue flowers with a deeper blue stripe on each petal. It grows to 6in (15cm) in height and, like so many bulbs, is best planted in groups.

ABOVE *Scilla mischtschenkoana*

NAME: *SISYRINCHIUM STRIATUM*

Origin: Australia, New Zealand, Hawaiian Islands, North America and Ireland
Type: Rhizomatous perennials
USDA Zone: Z8
Preferred pH range: 6.5–8.0
Description: The sword leaves of this robust plant are like those of *Iris*, and of about the same height; whorls of creamy flowers are produced in late summer when the quantity of other seasonal garden flowers is starting to decline. Each petal is striped brown. Although attractive, this plant can self-seed extensively, particularly in a sunny place. It looks particularly good, for some reason, when grown in gravel.
Popular species and varieties: *Sisyrinchium striatum* 'Aunt May' has leaves striped with cream; it is less vigorous than the plain species, but still flowers freely. *S. angustifolium* (known as the blue-eyed grass) carries little fans of leaves and bright blue flowers. It is perfect for small plantings on a rockery.

ABOVE *Sisyrinchium striatum*

ZANTEDESCHIA AETHIOPECA AGM (ARUM LILY or CALLA LILY)

Origin: South Africa
Type: Tuberous perennial
USDA Zone: Z8
Preferred pH range: 6.5–8.0
Description: This is a moisture-lover and can be grown in mild places in a sheltered border, or even as a marginal plant at the edge of a pond. The bright green arrow- to triangular-shaped leaves may reach up to 18in (45cm) long, held on strong stems. The pure white waxy flowers – which can be up to 10in (25cm) across – add grace and charm to any summer garden.

Popular species and varieties: *Zantedeschia aethiopeca* 'Apple Court Babe' is shorter and more compact than the species; 'Crowborough' AGM is hardier, more tolerant of drier conditions and has larger white spathes; 'Green Goddess' AGM has green markings on the white spathes, and is arguably hardier still; and 'Mr Martin' has probably the largest white spathes of all. Non-white zantedeschias are popular these days, but they tend to need winter protection, and are generally fussier plants. *Z. rehmanii* AGM (the pink arum) has pale pink spathes and *Z. elliottiana* AGM (the golden arum lily) has yellow spathes and spotted foliage.

ABOVE *Zantedeschia aethiopeca* AGM

BULBOUS PLANTS PREFERRING SOILS IN THE NEUTRAL RANGE

The following plants thrive in a soil with a pH range that straddles both the higher levels of acidity and the lower levels of alkalinity

Latin name	Common name	pH range
Amaryllis	Belladonna lily	5.5–7.5
Canna	Indian shot plant	6.0–7.5
Cardiocrinum	Giant lily	5.5–7.5
Chionodoxa	Glory of the snow	5.5–8.0
Crinum	Swamp lily	5.5–8.0
Dahlia	–	6.0–7.5
Erythronium	Dog's tooth violet	6.5–7.5
Freesia	–	6.0–8.0
Fritillaria	Fritillary/Crown imperial	6.0–7.5
Galtonia	Summer hyacinth/Spire lily	6.0–7.5
Hyacinthoides	Bluebell	6.0–7.5
Hyacinthus	Hyacinth	6.0–7.5
Leucojum	Snowflake	6.0–7.5
Muscari	Grape hyacinth	6.0–7.5
Nerine	Guernsey lily	6.5–7.5
Ornithogalum	Star of Bethlehem/Chincherinchee	6.5–7.5
Puschkinia	Little squill	5.5–8.0
Ranunculus	Buttercup	5.5–7.5
Rhodohypoxis	Rose grass	5.5–7.5
Schizostylis	Kaffir lily	5.5–7.5
Tecophilaea	–	6.5–7.5
Tigridia	Tiger flower	6.5–7.5
Tulipa	Tulip	6.0–7.5

ABOVE *Hyacinthoides hispanica*

ABOVE *Leucojum aestivum*

ABOVE *Cardiocrinum giganteum* AGM

PERENNIALS

NAME: *ACHILLEA* (YARROW)

Origin: Throughout the Northern Hemisphere
USDA Zone: Z3–5
Preferred pH range: 6.5–8.5
Description: *Achillea* flowerheads are composed of masses of tiny daisy-like flowers, loosely or tightly packed together into clusters or flat heads. There are many cultivars, with colours ranging from white through to the deepest red. The herbaceous border is the place for the larger species and cultivars, whilst the rock garden is suited to the smaller types. Sometimes the flowers can fade as they age.

Popular species and varieties: Most garden cultivars sit within the species *Achillea millefolium*. Look for 'Alabaster' (pale yellow fading to white); 'Belle Epoque' (opening red with yellowish streaks, fading to lemon yellow and pink); and 'Feuerland' (opening bright reddish orange, fading attractively – but unevenly – to orange and yellow). Apart from yellows, of which forms of *Achillea filipendulina* and the closely related 'Coronation Gold' AGM are unbeatable, the relatively new Summer Pastels achilleas have seen all their predecessors off. The flat flowerheads of most achilleas look best when not staked and allowed to flop. *A. ptarmica* 'The Pearl', however, should be staked; it has delightful pure white, rounded double flowers.

NAME: *ANEMONE X HYBRIDA* (JAPANESE ANEMONE)

Origin: Worldwide
USDA Zone: Z6
Preferred pH range: 6.0–8.5
Description: If you want flower colour in the garden from late summer to late autumn, then you would be well advised to grow a few Japanese anemones. Once planted these useful, long-lived hardy perennials can be left undisturbed for years, eventually building up into sizeable clumps. They are happiest in light shade and cope well with soils as high as pH8.0 (but note that bulbous and spring-flowering anemones prefer neutral to slightly acid conditions).

Popular species and varieties: Varieties of *Anemone* x *hybrida* can frequently be difficult to distinguish from varieties of *A. hupehensis*. The best advice is to trust a dependable nursery to supply the correct plants. The following represent some of the best varieties I've seen and are worth searching for. *A.* x *hybrida* 'Whirlwind' is a semi-double white form; 'Königin Charlotte' AGM is semi-double and pink; and 'Monterosa' is one of the best forms with large soft rose-pink flowers. *A. hupehensis* 'Bowles' Pink' AGM has varying shades of pink; 'Hadspen Abundance' AGM is purple-pink, with flowers some 2in (5cm) across; and 'Splendens' is a delightful bright purple-pink.

ABOVE *Achillea* 'Feuerland'

ABOVE *Anemone* 'Hadspen Abundance' AGM

NAME: *ARTEMESIA* (WORMWOOD)

Origin: Throughout the temperate regions of the Northern Hemisphere

USDA Zone: Z4–5

Preferred pH range: 6.5–8.0

Description: Although many will consider these to be shrubs, their wood is very light and some might well be better referred to as sub-shrubs. They can sometimes be on the tender side, too. They are grown for their soft, filigreed foliage that varies in the 'silveriness' of its grey, sometimes inclining towards a blue cast that is very attractive.

They are easy to grow, especially if you have a light, well-drained soil. The most important thing is that they should be grown in a sunny position.

Popular species and varieties: Look out for *Artemesia ludoviciana* 'Silver Queen' AGM, the slightly taller *A. absinthium* 'Lambrook Silver' AGM at 3ft (90cm) and the hybrid 'Powis Castle' AGM, with very finely cut foliage. *A. arborescens* 'Faith Raven' is a woody perennial with very finely cut silver-blue leaves. *A. ludoviciana* var. *latiloba* has foliage that is almost white.

ABOVE *Artemesia ludoviciana* 'Silver Queen' AGM

NAME: *ASTER* (MICHAELMAS DAISY)

Origin: Southeast Europe
USDA Zone: Z2–5
Preferred pH range: 6.5–8.5
Description: Michaelmas daisies are classic autumn flowers for gardens large and small. The blooms are beloved of bees and butterflies, making them even more welcome. Unfortunately these plants can also cause more disappointment than almost any other group of perennials. They suffer badly from mildew, and some years they can be a complete blot on many an otherwise fine garden landscape. There are also far too many varieties. However, when growing well, they brighten up a garden in early autumn like no other plant. They prefer an alkaline soil, and positively demand good soil drainage, especially in winter.

Popular species and varieties: *Aster frikartii* has a long flowering season, and an airy elegance that is entirely missing from the dumpy Michaelmas daisies. Varieties named after Swiss mountains are the ones to look out for, but never turn down an aster with the hybrid name alone. *A. amellus* 'King George' is a lovely pale purple. *A. novi-belgii* is also known as the New York aster, and my two favourite varieties are 'Little Pink Beauty' (with bright mauve-pink flowers on strong stems) and 'Professor Anton Kippenberg' (a reliable grower with lavender-blue flowers). The white heath aster (*A. ericoides*) produces a neat clump of large numbers of tiny flowers, bringing gentle colour into the later days of autumn. The form 'Golden Spray' AGM has small white flowers, each with a deep golden centre.

ABOVE *Aster* 'Little Pink Beauty'

NAME: *ASTRANTIA* (MASTERWORT)

Origin: Central and Eastern Europe
USDA Zone: Z6
Preferred pH range: 6.5–8.0
Description: These plants are particularly well suited to naturalistic gardens and shady corners. They have curiously shaped flowers comprising a dome of tiny florets surrounded by narrow, parchment-like bracts. This gives them a star-like appearance. All forms flower from late spring to early autumn.

Popular species and varieties: *Astrantia major* has starry, greenish-white flowers on stems 24in (60cm) high. There are a number of very good varieties, including 'Claret' (deep, rich pink), 'Ruby Wedding' (deep red) and 'Shaggy' (extra large bracts of white, tipped green). 'Sunningdale Variegated' has leaves with white streaks; it is very effective early in the season, as the streaks fade when the flowers start to appear. *Astrantia maxima* AGM is, to some, the best species as its flowers are a lovely rose-pink with striking emerald green on the underside. However, this is also a vigorous plant, and needs controlling. The hybrid *A.* 'Hadspen Blood' is a lovely deep reddish purple.

ABOVE *Astrantia major* 'Sunningdale Variegated'

NAME: *CONVALLARIA* (LILY-OF-THE-VALLEY)

Origin: Northern Europe
USDA Zone: Z3
Preferred pH range: 6.5–8.0
Description: Much loved for its exquisitely scented, little bell-shaped spring flowers, *Convallaria majalis* AGM makes good ground cover by early summer when its mid-green leaves are at their most voluminous; some people might think of this as being uncomfortably vigorous. It is considered to be a woodland plant as it is happiest in part shade, but sometimes almost full shade is tolerated. They will also tolerate full sun, if the summers are cool and the soil is steadily moist. The flowers are carried on elegant arching stems and open just above the foliage, or are sometimes partly hidden by it. The flowers are followed in summer and autumn by small scarlet berries.

Popular species and varieties: *Convallaria majalis* 'Albostriata' has leaves striped lengthways creamy-white; 'Dorien' has large flowers on long stems up to 12in (30cm) high; 'Flore Pleno' has double flowers; 'Prolificans' has branching flowerheads, and the blooms can sometimes be curiously misshapen; 'Variegata' has leaves with gold lengthways stripes; and *C. majalis* var. *rosea* has flowers of light mauve-pink.

ABOVE *Convallaria majalis* AGM

ABOVE *Crambe maritima* AGM

ABOVE *Cynara cardunculus*

NAME: *CRAMBE*

Origin: Europe, Asia and Tropical Africa
USDA Zone: Z5
Preferred pH range: 6.5–8.0
Description: Related to the common cabbage, these are easily grown perennials enjoying a sunny spot. A central crown and a mound of large, rounded, or lobed deciduous leaves emerge from deep, fleshy roots below ground. These leaves are handsome and textured, and are accompanied throughout summer by a glorious abundance of small white flowers.
Popular species and varieties: *Crambe cordifolia* AGM needs plenty of space for its robust clumps of foliage can reach some 5ft (1.5m) or more across. *C. maritima* AGM (more familiarly known as seakale) has rich purple shoots throughout spring, developing into undulating blue-grey foliage.

NAME: *CYNARA CARDUNCULUS* (CARDOON)

Origin: Canary Islands and the Mediterranean region
USDA Zone: Z6
Preferred pH range: 6.5–8.0
Description: A statuesque, sun-loving plant, this looks good in a border surrounded by other plants, or as a specimen plant on its own. A thistle-like, deciduous perennial, it has huge, spiny-margined leaves covered in tiny white hairs. The large violet-blue thistle-like flowerheads open in summer and early autumn.
Popular species and varieties: Only this species is commonly available, but look out for the cultivar 'Florist Cardy', with extra large flowerheads that are good for cutting and bringing indoors. Note that *C. cardunculus* Scolymus Group is another name for the globe artichoke (therefore better placed in the vegetable or kitchen garden), which grows best in the pH range 6.5–7.5.

NAME: *DIANTHUS* (CARNATIONS AND PINKS)

Origin: Throughout Europe and Asia

USDA Zone: Z3

Preferred pH range: 6.5–8.5

Description: This is a large genus of perennials (as well as annuals and biennials), at home in the border, the rockery, containers and even as greenhouse pot plants. All of the perennial forms are evergreen (often with greyish leaves). Flower colours are variously in shades from white to deep mauve, and every shade of pink and red in between – there are no oranges, yellows or blues. Border carnations are the hardiest, and often have quite large flowers. Modern and border pinks are daintier, and with the serrated edges to the petals (looking as if they have been gone over with a pair of 'pinking shears', the sort used in dressmaking). 'Mule pinks' are hybrids of the sweet william (see page 87).

Popular species and varieties: Modern pinks include 'Becky Robinson' AGM (with strongly clove-scented flowers of rose-pink with crimson zones); 'Doris' (pink, double and fragrant); and 'Haytor White' AGM (glistening white). Old-fashioned pinks include 'Mrs Sinkins' (white, double) and 'Dad's Favourite' (red and white, semi-double). *D. amurensis* has an endearing if lax habit, with large flowers in proportion to the plant; my favourite form is 'Siberian Blue', which is more mauve, with maroon centres to the flowers. For the rock garden try *Dianthus alpinus*, with deep pink or reddish flowers, and 'La Barboule' with scented pink flowers.

ABOVE *Dianthus* 'Becky Robinson' AGM

NAME: *DICENTRA (BLEEDING HEART)*

Origin: North America and Asia
USDA Zone: Z5
Preferred pH range: 7.0–8.0
Description: These are shade-loving perennials, whose elegant leaves and stems of heart-shaped flowers light up a darkish corner of the garden in spring. The foliage is prettily divided, making a pleasing background for the dangling flowers, which range in colour from pink, red and purple to yellow and white. They will often self-seed, giving highly variable seedlings; rogue them out, or deadhead the plants regularly, to keep plants true to type.
Popular species and varieties: The true bleeding heart is *Dicentra spactabilis* AGM, with elegant, tight clumps of light green leaves, finely lobed or divided. Flowers of rose-pink to purple-pink, with white 'lockets' (the 'droplets' at the bases of the flowers) are carried in long, arching sprays. 'Alba' AGM is pure white and 'Gold Heart' has yellow leaves and pale pink flowers. The hybrid 'Bacchanal' AGM is a lovely crimson, whilst *D. scandens* is a climbing form (perfect to ramble through large shrubs and over trelliswork) with yellow or sometimes white flowers.

NAME: *ERODIUM (HERON'S BILL)*

Origin: Europe and Central Asia, North Africa, North and South America and the cooler parts of Australia
USDA Zone: Z6–8
Preferred pH range: 7.0–8.0
Description: Valued for the long flowering period in summer, these are hardy, sun-loving perennials closely related to the *Geranium*. Some are most suited to rock or scree gardens, or troughs, but the larger types are better in mixed or herbaceous borders. They have rounded, five-petalled flowers in pink, purple, red, white or yellow.
Popular species and varieties: *Erodium manescaui* is a clump-forming plant, ideal for the front of a border. Clusters of saucer-shaped flowers in magenta-purple are freely produced on long stems. *E. pelargoniiflorum* (white), *E. chrysanthum* (cream) and *E. carvifolium* (red) are also worth searching for. Forms of *E. reichardii* are known as 'alpine geraniums', for they are at their best in rockeries. Look for 'Rubrum' (pink) and 'Album' (white).

ABOVE *Dicentra spectabilis* 'Alba' AGM

ABOVE *Erodium reichardii* 'Rubrum'

NAME: *ERYNGIUM* (ERYNGO or SEA HOLLY)

Origin: Worldwide
USDA Zone: Z3–5
Preferred pH range: 6.5–8.5
Description: These plants are striking and distinctive, with thistle-like flowers. There is nothing quite like them; their electric blue is perhaps at its best in the largest-flowered form – *Eryngium alpinum* AGM. These hardy plants have become very popular, and a well-grown specimen stands out well in any border. Taller kinds need staking.

Popular species and varieties: *Eryngium alpinum* AGM has flowerheads like small teasels, surrounded by prickly bracts and set on stout stems, all of the same distinctive colour. *E. x oliverianum* AGM reaches 2ft (60cm) and has large flowers for the genus. It has excellent contrasting qualities between the stiff foliage and steel-blue flowerheads. *E. planum* has an unfortunate tendency to sprawl, but it does introduce a diamond-blue shade that is hard to match. This form is excellent for cutting, having many smallish flowers on each stem. Of the hybrids, look for 'Jos Eijking'; it is very floriferous and very reliable. *E. giganteum* AGM has the common name of Miss Willmott's Ghost, and reaches a height of 5ft (1.5m); it has a definite value in the garden, but is a short-lived perennial, lasting perhaps only two seasons.

NAME: *GERANIUM* (CRANESBILL)

Origin: Northeastern Turkey
USDA Zone: Z6
Preferred pH range: 6.0–8.5
Description: These plants will grow well in sun or shade – a rare thing! The misapplied common name for the bedding geranium (more properly *Pelargonium*) certainly needs a position in full sun, and this is perhaps where the sun-loving reputation for any plants with the name 'Geranium' has arisen. Nearly all of these perennials are clump-formers, making them best suited to the front of borders, but they also make a good show of themselves in containers. Most will also withstand summer drought conditions.

Popular species and varieties: *Geranium sanguineum* (known as the bloody cranesbill) forms a low mat of small, divided, rounded leaves, topped by large numbers of purple-magenta flowers over a long period. *G. sanguineum* var. *striatum* AGM has graceful, light pink petals delicately veined with a deeper pink. *G. psilostemon* AGM has bright magenta flowers and can easily reach 4ft (1.2m) in height, so unusually for a *Geranium* is better mid-way or at the back of a border. The lavender-blue hybrid 'Nimbus' AGM is extremely vigorous, free-flowering and is an excellent ground-cover plant.

ABOVE *Eryngium giganteum* AGM

ABOVE *Geranium 'Nimbus'* AGM

NAME: *HELENIUM* (SNEEZEWEED)

Origin: North and Central America
USDA Zone: Z3
Preferred pH range: 6.5–8.0
Description: Predominately plants with daisy flowers in shades of yellow, they do make a bold statement. Fortunately they can bring a garden alive, as they flower in late summer and autumn, when there may be little else in colour. They are not really at home in the herbaceous border but look well among luscious green foliage and, perhaps, daisy flowers and others in the white to cream range. Despite the unfortunate sounding common name, these are valuable and worthwhile perennials. Most grow taller than 39in (1m).
Popular species and varieties: Look for the following cultivars: 'Butterpat' AGM (pale yellow), 'Moerheim Beauty' AGM (bronze red), 'Crimson Beauty' (mahogany brown), 'Coppelia' (coppery orange), 'Kanaria' (bright, clean yellow) and 'Wyndley' (deep yellow with brown-red streaks).

NAME: *HELIANTHUS* (PERENNIAL SUNFLOWER)

Origin: North and South America
USDA Zone: Z4–7
Preferred pH range: 7.0–8.0
Description: These are tough, reliable plants, all with cheery yellow daisy flowerheads; some are coarse and invasive, but many are well behaved. These are ideal subjects for providing late summer colour in the border. The taller types need staking, and it is a good idea to deadhead regularly to prevent the plants self-seeding (which results in different and confusing seedlings).
Popular species and varieties: Several hybrids are worth growing. Look for: 'Lemon Queen' AGM, with pale yellow flowers that stand out well from the deep green, hairy leaves; 'Miss Mellish' AGM and 'Loddon Gold' AGM have large flowers of deep yellow; a gentler yellow is provided by 'Capenoch Star' AGM. 'Morgensonne' (sometimes labelled as 'Morning Sun') has very uniform flowers of bright yellow. The annual sunflower (*Helianthus annuus*) is popular as a garden plant and for cut flowers.

ABOVE *Helenium* 'Wyndley'

ABOVE *Helianthus* 'Morgensonne'

NAME: *HELLEBORUS* (HELLEBORE)

Origin: Western and Central Europe, Russia
USDA Zone: Z3–6
Preferred pH range: 7.0–8.5
Description: Hellebores are fashionable winter and spring plants, and are now available in a huge range of forms, colours and patterns. They are addictive, such is their magic, especially the hybrids of *Helleborus* x *hybridus* (the Lenten rose). But these are by no means the only members of the family. Most hellebores will grow in full sun or light shade, but at all costs you should avoid growing them in places that are exposed to cold winds. They are happiest in alkaline to neutral soils.
Popular species and varieties: The Oriental Hybrids are the most popular; there are a great many named varieties in a wide range of colours from almost black to purple, yellow, pink and white, some with plain flowers, others spotted and veined. Garden centres stock a good range, and it is best to see the plants in flower before making your choice. The Christmas rose (*H. niger* AGM) has flat pure white flowers, occasionally with pinkish tones. The stinking hellebore (*H. foetidus*), so-called because of the unpleasant smell coming from the foliage when crushed, is particularly useful for lightly shaded areas. It has pale green flowers and is a real beauty. Among the named forms is the Wester Flisk Group, with reddish stems.

ABOVE *Helleborus orientalis*

NAME: *HEUCHERA* (ALUM ROOT or CORALBELLS)

Origin: North America
USDA Zone: Z4–9
Preferred pH range: 7.0–8.0
Description: These are neat evergreen perennials, giving all-year-round interest. Because so much breeding work has taken place with *Heuchera* over the past ten years or so there are an increasing number of varieties to choose from. Grown primarily for their attractive leaves, the wispy flowers on wiry stems are of secondary importance. All are mound-forming plants.
Popular species and varieties: Most of the garden-worthy varieties today are hybrids. Look for 'Amber Waves' (yellow and bronze leaves), 'Amethyst Mist' (burgundy and silver), 'Frosted Violet' (pinkish violet leaves mottled silver in the spring, becoming bronze-purple in summer), 'Chocolate Ruffles' (red-purple-chocolate brown leaves) and 'Palace Purple Select' (bronze leaves and white flowers).

ABOVE *Heuchera* 'Frosted Violet'

ABOVE *Lamium* 'White Nancy' AGM

ABOVE *Paeonia* 'Miss America'

NAME: *LAMIUM* (DEADNETTLE)

Origin: Mediterranean
USDA Zone: Z3–6
Preferred pH range: 6.5–8.0
Description: A useful hardy perennial for ground cover, the most widely grown forms are varieties of *Lamium maculatum*, the spotted dead nettle. It is successful particularly in shaded spots under large trees. The straight species has green foliage, each leaf having a silver stripe down the middle. It also carries deep, purplish-pink flowers from late spring to late summer. It much prefers a moist soil.
Popular species and varieties: Among the numerous varieties available are 'Aureum' (golden leaves and pink flowers); 'Beacon Silver' (silvery foliage and bright, deep pink flowers); 'Pink Pewter' (leaves of silver-green, edged green, and flowers of salmon-pink); 'White Nancy' AGM (white flowers and silver leaves); and 'Roseum' (very pale pink flowers and leaves with a central silver stripe).

NAME: *PAEONIA* (PEONY)

Origin: Asia mainly, with some forms coming from Europe and America
USDA Zone: Z5–8
Preferred pH range: 7.0–8.5
Description: Peonies are beautiful and elegant spring-and-summer perennials, for borders and for cutting. Forms of herbaceous peonies (as opposed to the shrubby, woody forms) are long-term plants that will do well if left alone, provided that they are started with every advantage in terms of well-drained soil and plenty of well-rotted compost. Only when they stop flowering abundantly should they be lifted, divided, and replanted, again with plenty of nutriment. Peonies enjoy heat and will thrive on thin, chalky soils as long as they are well fed. Growth is slow in the first year after planting, and it speeds up until the optimum flowering, usually in the fourth year.
Popular species and varieties: *Paeonia lactiflora* is the parent plant to many modern peony hybrids.

They are often very showy and the flowers can be heavy enough to need staking. They are also known as the Chinese peonies. The range of colours is huge. There are some singles, but the greater part of the range consists of doubles and the very beautiful imperials, whose flowers have an outer ring of large petals, which enclose a neat mass of inner petals. Arguably the best (but there are hundreds of cultivars to choose from) is 'Bowl of Beauty' AGM, rose-pink outer petals and deep cream inner petaloids, but 'Kelway's Majestic', magenta, with a yellow centre, and 'Miss America', cream-white and semi-double, are good too. *P. cambessedesii* AGM is a species with beautiful foliage of deep green, with red stalks and leaf-reverses, and large, rose-pink flowers. It is rather tender, so if you live in a cool region it definitely requires the warmest, sunniest part of the garden. *P. mlokosewitschii* AGM is a lovely, yellow flowered peony. It is, not surprisingly, known as 'Molly the Witch'. The blooms are large and of a light but substantial lemon yellow. *P. officinalis* is the species with several superb hybrids, the best to my mind being 'Lize van Veen' (pink and white, double) and 'Rubra Plena' AGM (deep purplish red, double).

NAME: *PULMONARIA* (LUNGWORT)

Origin: Europe
USDA Zone: Z3–6
Preferred pH range: 6.5–8.5
Description: The small, five-petalled flowers on these plants are familiar in spring gardens, and later the typically spotted leaves make a pleasing addition to shady borders. There are ten species, all of which are small herbaceous plants with short flower stems. Leaves are usually oval or oblong, never divided, and are usually roughly hairy, like all parts of the plant. The foliage may be green or marked with silvery spots and blotches. Pulmonarias go by a number of common names, including lungworts,

Josephs and Maries, the Good Friday plant, thunder and lightning, soldiers and sailors, and Jerusalem sage (not to be confused with the yellow-flowering shrub, *Phlomis fruticosa*).

Popular species and varieties: *Pulmonaria saccharata* is an attractive plant from France and Italy and has large leaves that are heavily spotted, and leafy flower stems with purplish blooms. The best cultivars are those with the most silvered leaves, which include the 'Argentea Group' AGM. The hybrid 'Roy Davidson' has narrow leaves, lightly spotted in silver; its flowers are mid-blue fading to pink. 'Mawson's Blue' has plain unspotted green leaves with rich, dark blue flowers appearing in mid-spring. *P. angustifolia* AGM has plain, pale green leaves, which emerge early and contrast well with the mid-blue flowers. *P. angustifolia* 'Munstead Blue' is widely available and has light green, unspotted leaves and bright blue flowers.

ABOVE *Pulmonaria* 'Roy Davidson'

NAME: *SAXIFRAGA* (SAXIFRAGE)

Origin: Worldwide, most frequently in mountainous zones
USDA Zone: Z3–7
Preferred pH range: 7.0–8.0
Description: A large genus comprising around 400 species, these are some of our most familiar rockery and alpine plants. Most of the small alpine saxifrages are sun-lovers, but there are larger species that are becoming more widely grown, and which are perfect for the front of shady beds and borders. More important than the light, however, is that the soil should always be moist – not wet – but moist. The plants will die quickly if allowed to get dry, and if they languish in wet soil for too long.
Popular species and varieties: *Saxifraga fortunei* is a glossy, leafy plant. Dainty white, star-shaped blooms are carried in airy masses on long stems in late autumn. The variety 'Black Ruby' has almost black leaves and pink flowers. *S. 'Stansfieldii'* produces lovely rose-pink flowers with yellow-green centres. The plant commonly known as mother-of-thousands (*S. stolonifera*) is often grown as a house plant, but it will in fact grow outside in sheltered positions, where it will form an attractive ground-cover plant, its evergreen oval leaves spreading freely.

ABOVE *Saxifraga 'Stansfieldii'*

NAME: *SILENE* (CAMPION OR CATCHFLY)

Origin: Throughout the Northern Hemisphere, frequently around coastal regions
USDA Zone: Z3–6
Preferred pH range: 7.0–8.0
Description: If you desire a natural-looking garden, then plant some silenes, for these look like wild plants – but much more decorative. The *Silene* genus is large, with some 500 species of annuals, biennials and deciduous or evergreen perennials. Most are mat-forming plants, and they are easily grown with flowers in a range of hues from white to deep pink.
Popular species and varieties: *Silene acaulis* develops into a neat, rounded plant with pale pink flowers. *S. uniflora* (known as the sea campion) is a woody, semi-evergreen form with showy white flowers; in the cultivar 'Druett's Variegated' the leaves have thick cream margins with a mid-green stripe along the centre.

ABOVE *Silene acaulis*

NAME: *STACHYS* (LAMB'S EAR)

Origin: Southwest Asia
USDA Zone: Z5
Preferred pH range: 6.5–8.0
Description: These are mostly spreading perennials, making colourful and valuable ground cover in a range of situations. The well-known lamb's tongue (sometimes lamb's ears) is an ideal carpeting plant with densely silvery-woolly leaves. *Stachys* rarely reaches higher than 12in (30cm). The hairy-leaved kinds prefer a position in full sun; the others do not mind so much moisture, and tolerate light shade.

Popular species and varieties: The best form for most gardens is *Stachys byzantina* 'Silver Carpet', as it does not flower. Flowering is a distraction and it spoils the ground-covering effect. 'Silky Fleece' is a recent introduction that does have rather attractive, chunky, lavender-like flowers. The scarlet hedgenettle (*S. coccinea*) is a semi-shrubby evergreen perennial with upright scarlet flowers appearing sporadically from mid-spring to mid-autumn.

ABOVE *Stachys coccinea*

ABOVE *Stachys byzantina*

117

PERENNIAL PLANTS PREFERRING SOILS IN THE NEUTRAL RANGE

The following plants thrive in a soil with a pH range that straddles both the higher
levels of acidity and the lower levels of alkalinity

Latin name	Common name	pH range
Adonis	–	6.0–7.5
Bletilla	Hardy orchid	6.0–7.5
Cerastium	Snow-in-summer	6.0–7.5
Corynephorus	Hair grass	5.5–7.5
Dactylorhiza	Marsh orchid	5.5–7.5
Epimedium	Barrenwort	6.0–7.5
Eremurus	Foxtail lily	6.0–8.0
Euphorbia	Spurge	6.0–7.5
Glaucidium	–	6.0–7.5
Gymnocarpium	Oak fern	5.5–7.5
Jeffersonia	Twin leaf	5.5–7.5
Knautia	–	6.5–7.5
Mimulus	Monkey flower/Musk flower	6.0–7.5
Phlegopteris	Beech fern	5.5–7.5
Roscoea	–	5.5–7.5
Scabiosa	Pincushion flower/Scabious	6.0–8.0
Schoenoplectus	Bullrush/Club rush	5.5–7.5
Semiaquilegia	–	6.0–7.5
Solidago	Golden rod	5.5–7.5
Veronica	Speedwell	5.5–7.5

ABOVE *Euphorbia characias 'Lambrook Gold' AGM*

ABOVE *Dactylorhiza majalis*

TREES, SHRUBS AND CLIMBERS

NAME: *ABELIA*

Origin: China, Japan and the warmer parts of the Himalayas, Mexico

Type: Deciduous, semi-evergreen and evergreen shrubs

USDA Zone: Z5–8

Preferred pH range: 6.0–8.0

Description: The flowers of these shrubs are tubular to bell-shaped, and they can range from white through to red. If you look closely you can see a certain similarity to that of the honeysuckle flower, to which they are related. Individually, the flowers are rather small, but they come in their hundreds, and over a long period in summer and the first half of autumn.

Popular species and varieties: *A. grandiflora* 'Francis Mason' has white flowers, and the leaves are flushed orange when young. 'Gold Spot' is also white, and the foliage is variegated with yellow. *A. schumannii* flowers from early summer through to mid-autumn, with bright pink flowers. *A.* 'Edward Goucher' has lavender pink flowers with glossy, semi-evergreen foliage.

ABOVE *Abelia grandiflora* 'Francis Mason'

NAME: *AESCULUS* (HORSE CHESTNUT or BUCKEYE)

Origin: North America, Europe, eastern Asia

Type: Deciduous trees and shrubs

USDA Zone: Z4–8

Preferred pH range: 7.0–8.0

Description: The horse chestnut (*Aesculus hippocastanum* AGM) is happy on dry, alkaline soil, and is often self-seeding. There is nothing quite like their candelabra-flowers in early summer and, pink- and red-flowered varieties exist. *Aesculus* is also familiar for its autumn fruits – the 'conkers' so beloved by children for the schoolyard games. But this tree grows to more than 30ft (9m) in ten years. However, there are a few smaller ones worth considering.

Popular species and varieties: *Aesculus pavia* AGM has interesting coral-red flowers opening slightly. *A. parviflora* AGM will reach just 10ft (3m) or so, and is a valuable white-flowering tall shrub for late summer. The red horse chestnut (*A.* x *carnea*) reaches a height of 20ft (6m) after ten years. Although called 'red', its flowers are actually pink. It is best in the form 'Briottii' AGM.

ABOVE *Aesculus* x *carnea*

119

NAME: *BERBERIS* (BARBERRY)

Origin: Temperate parts worldwide
Type: Deciduous and evergreen shrubs
USDA Zone: Z3–8
Preferred pH range: 6.5–8.0
Description: This is a large genus, of which all plants produce masses of yellow, orange or red flowers that appear, mainly, during early spring. There are deciduous types, and these mostly need full sun; the evergreen species are happier in dappled to light shade. Even better, these are undemanding shrubs – easy to grow and with no major pest and disease problems. The only word of warning is to watch out for their often vicious thorns, which does make them ideal as barrier or hedging plants.
Popular species and varieties: *B. thunbergii* f. *atropurpurea* is impossibly prickly, with deep purple leaves throughout the spring and summer, and which in autumn turn a fiery orange-red, with little glossy berries. *B. linearifolia* 'Orange King' has deep orange flowers; *B.* x *stenophylla* 'Claret Cascade' has red-orange flowers, whilst 'Corallina Compacta' AGM has coral pink flowers. The best of them all, to my mind, is *B. darwinii* AGM; vivid orange flowers appear in late winter and spring, accompanied by the small, neat glossy evergreen leaves.

ABOVE *Berberis darwinii* **AGM**

NAME: *BETULA* (BIRCH)

Origin: Temperate and Arctic regions throughout the Northern Hemisphere
Type: Deciduous trees and shrubs
USDA Zone: Z1–7
Preferred pH range: 6.5–8.0
Description: The common silver birch (*Betula pendula* AGM) is the best of the birches, and takes fairly dry conditions. It can be grown as a specimen or in a group of three or five (if you have the room); it looks beautiful in winter with the black and white trunks and the gently weeping, dark red shoots moving in the wind. Bulbs (crocuses, snowdrops and bluebells) can be very successfully grown under them.
Popular species and varieties: *Betula pendula* AGM is the most familiar of the birches, the form 'Dalecarlica' has a more upright habit with pendant, shorter shoots at the ends of the branches, and much more deeply cut leaves. *B. utilis* var. *jacquemontii* is widely regarded by many as having the brightest white of any tree bark – certainly it does take some beating.

ABOVE *Betula utilis* var. *jacquemontii*

NAME: *BUDDLEJA* (BUTTERFLY BUSH)

Origin: China, Japan and South America
Type: Deciduous and evergreen shrubs
USDA Zone: Z5–7
Preferred pH range: 6.5–8.5
Description: Everyone knows the butterfly bush, *Buddleja davidii*, which when in full flower is invaded seemingly by thousands of butterflies. It's long violet and purple flower spikes, arching gracefully out and away from the base, are a real joy of the mid- to late-summer garden. If it has a chance, it will self-seed, and these seedlings can pop up in the most unlikely of places, including house guttering, cracks in paving and walls and, obviously, on any piece of ground within throwing distance of the main plant. This all goes to suggest that buddlejas are both prodigious, and also unfussy as to the growing conditions. But without fail, if you have a chalky soil with a pH of 7.5 and slightly higher, these plants will be most at home. All flowers are fragrant, either slightly or powerfully. Prune buddlejas in winter, to several inches from the ground.

Popular species and varieties: *Buddleja davidii* 'Black Knight' has dark violet-purple flowers; 'Empire Blue' AGM is blue-mauve, each tiny flower with an orange eye; 'Harlequin' is red-purple, with cream-variegated leaves; 'Peace' is white; and 'Royal Red' AGM is purple-red. *B. globosa* is the golden ball tree, because the flowerheads are bright orange, and about the size of a ping-pong ball, and quite unlike the main *Buddleja* portfolio.

ABOVE *Buddleja davidii* 'Empire Blue' AGM

NAME: *CISTUS* (ROCK ROSE or SUN ROSE)

Origin: Meditteranean region
Type: Evergreen shrubs
USDA Zone: Z7–8
Preferred pH range: 6.0–8.0
Description: Only plant this shrub if you have a sunny spot – otherwise it will surely fail. White is the principal flower colour, followed by pink, but most forms have petals marked with various blotches. Individual blooms have five wide-spreading petals that resemble those of the wild rose. The blooms last for just a day, sometimes just a morning with the petals all but gone by mid-afternoon. Fortunately the flowers come in such profusion that you hardly notice this.

Popular species and varieties: *Cistus* x *purpureus* AGM features masses of large, rich-pink flowers with maroon blotches on neat 4ft (1.2m) high stems. *C.* x *dansereaui* has saucer-shaped blooms of pure white, each with a central deep red blotch. *C. albidus* has lovely light pink flowers from late spring to mid-summer; however, this is not a long-lived plant, and a severe winter may cause its demise.

ABOVE *Cistus x purpureus* AGM

ABOVE *Clematis* 'Warsaw Nike'

NAME: *CLEMATIS*

Origin: Northern Europe, Russia
Type: Evergreen and deciduous climbers
USDA Zone: Z5
Preferred pH range: 6.0–8.0
Description: One of the most commonly held beliefs about *Clematis*, known as the 'queen of climbers', is that they must be grown on a chalky soil. This probably arises from *Clematis vitalba* (known as old man's beard, or traveller's joy); it is a species that occurs naturally on thin, chalky soils, and was traditionally used as a rootstock, onto which were grafted large-flowered hybrids. However, *Clematis* can usually survive reasonably well on neutral and even slightly acid soils, with plenty of moisture available, if well drained. Sandy soils drain too quickly for *Clematis* and heavy soils are too wet and cold in winter for fine-rooted varieties. There are some quite beautiful forms, and for almost every garden situation. The normal rule is that the 'top of the plant should be in the sun, and the roots should be in the shade', but it is fair to say that many of the popular summer-flowering hybrids offer their best flower-colour when the head of the plant is lightly shaded; intense sunlight can quickly fade and scorch the blooms.

Popular species and varieties: The hybrids are the most colourful members of the family, and one of my favourites is 'The President', with single flowers of rich purple, each petal having a faint silver stripe; the centre of the blooms comprises red anthers. 'Marie Boisselot' AGM is creamy-white with anthers of golden yellow. 'Ernest Markham' grows to 8ft (2.5m) and likes a sunny place. Its flowers are bright rose-pink and appear from early summer to early autumn. 'Vyvyan Pennell' has double flowers during the early part of the season, and single towards the latter; they are pale mauve, and hold their colour well in strong sunlight. 'Warsaw Nike' has rich velvety-red petals contrasting well with the pale yellow anthers.

The *Clematis montana* clan are valuable in that they do not need pruning, and one of the best is 'Elizabeth', with scented pink flowers. *C. armandii* 'Snowdrift' is the only evergreen clematis and is not reliably hardy, requiring a sheltered, sunny wall, and winter protection in cold districts. Its flowers are white, flat and appear in mid- to late spring.

NAME: *CRATAEGUS* (THORN, HAWTHORN or MAY)

Origin: Throughout the Northern Hemisphere
Type: Deciduous or rarely semi-evergreen trees and shrubs
USDA Zone: Z2–7
Preferred pH range: 7.0–8.5
Description: One of the most attractive small flowering trees of all time is the wild white form of *Crataegus monogyna*. It makes a domed crown with hanging branches that are wreathed with small clusters of white flowers; these flowers are followed by maroon-red berries in autumn (and these often persist long into winter). All the forms can be trained into trees, or they can be kept shrubby by regular pruning, if you prefer.
Popular species and varieties: One of the best

cultivars is *Crataegus monogyna* 'Biflora', sometimes known as the Glastonbury thorn. It produces some flowers during mild winter periods, in addition to its normal flush in late spring. *C.* x *lavalleei* 'Carrierei' AGM has leaves which persist into mid-winter, accompanied by orange-red fruits that can last almost until spring. The leaves of *C. persimilis* 'Prunifolia' AGM turn from glossy green to orange, then red and finally crimson in autumn.

ABOVE *Crataegus monogyna*

NAME: *DAPHNE*

Origin: Europe, North Africa, temperate Asia
Type: Deciduous and evergreen shrubs
USDA Zone: Z4–8
Preferred pH range: 7.0–8.5
Description: The scent of these flowers, wafting across the garden on a still winter's day, is like no other. The thick matt green leaves and the small whitish or pink flowers, and often the red berries as well are all attractive enough, but the fragrance will blow your socks off, and renders the *Daphne* essential planting near to a back door where, even during winter when occasional forays have to be made into the garden, it will be appreciated.

Popular species and varieties: *Daphne mezereum* is a chalk native, and it's a deciduous, small shrub with upright branches. Purple-red flowers are carried in mid-winter on the previous year's shoots; red berries follow. *D. odora* is a small, rounded, evergreen shrub with glossy, dark green leaves. Slightly hardier and more widely grown is *D. odora* 'Aureomarginata' AGM, with narrow, cream-yellow margins around the leaves. The star-shaped mauve-purple flowers, carried in clusters, are wonderfully fragrant. *D.* x *napolitana* 'Bramdean' has gorgeous large sugar-pink flowers but it marginally less scented.

NAME: *DEUTZIA* (BEAUTY BUSH)

Origin: Asia and Central America
Type: Deciduous shrubs
USDA Zone: Z4–8
Preferred pH range: 6.5–8.0
Description: Despite *Deutzia* being one of those easy-going summer flowering shrubs, it is rarely the first choice for gardeners. These are generally problem-free and very accommodating shrubs, but they are frequently planted too close in mixed borders and therefore seldom seen at their best. Both single- and double-flowered forms are available, with flower colour ranging from white through the shades of pink to carmine. Most deutzias have flowers that are fragrant. Flowers appear in late spring and early summer, and are carried in clusters.

Popular species and varieties: *Deutzia* x *kalmiiflora* is a beauty, carrying a mass of early summer flowers that are deep pink outside, white inside. *D. setchuenensis* var. *corymbiflora* AGM produces small starry white flowers appearing later in the season than most other deutzias; it is a little more tender than the other forms. There are several cultivars of *D.* x *hybrida*. Look for: 'Contraste' (large flowers with a deep purple band on the back of each petal) and 'Mont Rose' AGM (free-flowering, with rose-pink blooms, often tinted darker).

ABOVE ***Daphne x napolitana* 'Bramdean'**

ABOVE ***Deutzia x kalmiiflora***

NAME: *ELAEAGNUS* (OLEASTER)

Origin: North America, southern Europe and the Far East

Type: Evergreen and deciduous shrubs

USDA Zone: Z2–10

Preferred pH range: 5.0–8.0

Description: Many of the evergreen species have very rich leaf markings, with speckles of bright yellow, cream and even near-white, while the deciduous species generally have silvery leaves. The flowers are not particularly decorative, but they are highly fragrant. Most forms are fast growing, and the evergreen species are usefully tolerant of wind.

Popular species and varieties: Some of the slower-growing types, and therefore suitable for smaller gardens, include *E.* x *ebbingei* 'Gilt Edge' AGM, *E. pungens* 'Frederici' and *E. pungens* 'Maculata'. The frequently grown variegated cultivars such as 'Maculata' and *E.* x *ebbingei* 'Limelight', are a common sight in public schemes, from roadside to supermarket planting. This confirms their robust constitutions. And their colour is brightest in the deep, dark winter days when we need cheering up. Each leaf of *E.* x *ebbingei* Gold Splash (syn. 'Lannou') has a bright central splash of buttercup-yellow. With *E. pungens* 'Goldrim' AGM the green leaves each have a bright yellow margin; white flowers appear during autumn. It has a height and spread 6ft (2m) or so. Of the deciduous species, arguably the best known is 'Quicksilver'. It is, perhaps, one of the best silver broad-leaved shrubs available. Some species, including *Elaeagnus* x *ebbingei*, are larger-growing; this form can reach up to 15ft (5m). It also makes a good hedge as it is easy to keep in shape.

ABOVE *Elaeagnus pungens* 'Maculata'

NAME: *JUNIPERUS COMMUNIS* (COMMON JUNIPER)

Origin: Throughout the Northern Hemisphere
Type: Coniferous trees of varying sizes
USDA Zone: Z2–7
Preferred pH range: 6.5–8.0
Description: Many junipers are natives to chalk soils and will nearly always perform well on an alkaline soil – providing it does not get waterlogged, nor bone dry in summer. The 60 or more species in the genus have given us a multitude of shapes, forms and colours to suit almost any garden and climate. Most prefer sunny positions. The species varies so widely in habit, from narrowly columnar to bushy and prostrate, and many garden cultivars have been collected from the wild.
Popular species and varieties: The Noah's Ark juniper (*Juniperus communis* 'Compressa' AGM) forms a tightly compressed miniature column of light green. Another cultivar, 'Gold Cone', is very descriptive of the plant which bears this name. So too is 'Green Carpet' AGM. 'Hibernica' AGM is known as the Irish juniper and is a very narrow, upright form. 'Repanda' AGM is much used for ground cover, and is known for its bronze-green foliage in winter.

ABOVE *Juniperus communis* 'Compressa' AGM

NAME: *LABURNUM* (GOLDEN RAIN)

Origin: Southern Europe and the Middle East
Type: Deciduous trees
USDA Zone: Z5–6
Preferred pH range: 6.5–8.0
Description: These gorgeous spring-flowering beauties are so accommodating that they can be seen, almost certainly self-seeded, on waste ground in temperate parts of the world. The long golden racemes are beautiful in mid-spring, and the trees can cope with highly alkaline soil. These are not long-lived trees – by normal tree standards that is – but they will still give a fairly good account of themselves for around 40 years or so, if looked after.
Popular species and varieties: *Laburnum* x *watereri* reaches some 16–20ft (4–5m) after 20 years, *L. alpinum* is no less attractive, but rather smaller, with darker leaves.

ABOVE *Laburnum alpinum*

NAME: *LAVANDULA* (LAVENDER)

Origin: Mediterranean region, North Africa, western Asia, Arabia, India
Type: Evergreen shrubs
USDA Zone: Z5–9
Preferred pH range: 6.5–8.0
Description: Lavender is among the best known of all shrubs, valued primarily for its aromatic foliage and flowers. The 'lavender' comes from the lavender water that is made from the oil distilled from the plants; with *lavo* being latin for 'wash'. The silver foliage ensures that plants are decorative all year round.

Popular species and varieties: There is a host of excellent varieties, including 'Hidcote' AGM (violet flowers) and 'Hidcote Pink' (with pink flowers). 'Nana Alba' has white flowers and is a dwarf form at just 12in (30cm) high. The French lavender (*Lavandula stoechas* AGM) has become very popular in recent years. It has dark purple flowers borne in dense, congested heads topped by distinctive terminal bracts. The old English lavender (*L. angustifolia*) has pale blue flowers on long stems. A white form of it ('Alba') is available.

ABOVE *Lavandula stoechas* AGM

135

NAME: *LAVATERA* (TREE MALLOW)

Origin: The Mediterranean region, through Central Asia, Australia and western US

Type: Semi-evergreen shrubs and sub-shrubs

USDA Zone: Z8–9

Preferred pH range: 6.0–8.0

Description: Until the 1990s the shrubby mallow was generally offered as a herbaceous plant, and only a few soft, small specimens were sold each year. Since then its qualities have been recognized and it is now highly popular. It grows quickly, flowers for a long period and mixes well with herbaceous plants and shrubs alike. These plants are good on chalk, good for hot, sunny sites, and good in coastal gardens.

Popular species and varieties: Look for cultivars of *Lavatera* x *clementii*. 'Rosea' AGM has large pink flowers all up the stems from early summer until late autumn. 'Barnsley' is a sport of 'Rosea' with flowers of the palest pink, and each with a red eye. 'Blushing Bride' is more compact but with similar flowers. 'Burgundy Wine' AGM has deep purplish-pink flowers.

ABOVE *Lavatera x clementii* 'Rosea' AGM

NAME: *LIGUSTRUM* (PRIVET)

Origin: Europe, North Africa, southern Asia and Australia

Type: Deciduous and evergreen shrubs and trees

USDA Zone: Z3–8

Preferred pH range: 7.0–8.0

Description: Privet, regularly seen in chalkland hedgerows, is often despised, but the Victorians found it a wonderful plant, with its sweet, stuffy flowers in mid-summer and later black berries. When well fed, watered and generally cared for, it makes a good-looking hedge.

Popular species and varieties: *Ligustrum ovalifolium* is the usual plain green hedging plant. More attractive is *L. ovalifolium* 'Aureum' AGM with golden yellow leaves; this plant can also be grown successfully as a standard plant on its own. The cultivar 'Vicaryi', has lovely clear lime-green leaves.

ABOVE *Ligustrum* 'Vicaryi'

NAME: *PASSIFLORA* (PASSION FLOWER)

Origin: Brazil, Argentina, United States
Type: Evergreen and semi-evergreen tendril climbers
USDA Zone: Z7
Preferred pH range: 6.0–8.0
Description: The blue passion flower, *Passiflora caerulea* AGM, does well in alkaline soils, but succumbs to a tough winter. Grown in the soil of a greenhouse – even an unheated one – it will produce a continuous crop of incredible flowers. It is called the 'passion' flower in relation to the Passion of Christ. The blooms were used by the Jesuits in South America: the three stigmas being the three nails that held Christ on the cross, the five anthers were the five wounds, the corona was Christ's halo and the ten petals were the apostles (Peter and Judas being absent). There are several kinds of passion flower, of varying degrees of hardiness.

Popular species and varieties: 'Constance Elliott' is an ivory white variety with yellow anthers. The maypop (*P. incarnata*) is the hardiest species, with somewhat smaller flowers yet still showy; it is actually a perennial climber, dying to the ground in winter but rapidly growing the following year to reach 20ft (6m) or so by late summer. A lovely purple flower comes in the species *P. racemosa* AGM.

ABOVE *Passiflora caerulea* AGM

NAME: *SYRINGA (LILAC)*

Origin: Southeast Europe, eastern Asia
Type: Deciduous shrubs and trees
USDA Zone: Z4–6
Preferred pH range: 7.0–8.5
Description: Lilac shrubs (or trees) are most definitely for alkaline soils. Try growing them in anything under pH7.0 (neutral) and they will more than likely be most sickly. They are grown for their often pyramid or conical shaped flowerheads comprising many small, tubular and usually very fragrant flowers. These may be white, pink, almost red to magenta, blue or lilac (which is how the shade of light purplish-pink became so named).

Popular species and varieties: Most garden cultivars are grouped under *Syringa vulgaris.* Look for: 'Charles Joly' AGM (double, dark purple); 'Katherine Havemeyer' AGM (double, lavender-blue from purple buds); 'Mme Antoine Buchner' AGM (double, pale mauve-pink from dark purple-red buds); and 'Mont Blanc' (single, white). *S. meyeri* carries small clusters of bluish-pink flowers, and in the cultivar 'Palibin' AGM the lavender-pink clusters are more dense.

NAME: *VIBURNUM*

Origin: Temperate Northern Hemisphere, extending into South America and Malaysia
Type: Deciduous and evergreen shrubs
USDA Zone: Z2–9
Preferred pH range: 6.5–8.0
Description: This is a very large genus of shrubs, with some 150 species and many cultivars. It is a hugely versatile genus, and most forms are undemanding and easy to grow. Many are noted for their wonderful flower fragrances. Viburnums are most suited to shrub borders or woodland gardens, rather than as specimen shrubs growing on their own.

Popular species and varieties: *Viburnum tinus* flowers intermittently for eight or nine months of the year. Blooms are generally white with the merest hint of pink. 'Eve Price' is more compact-growing, and 'Gwenllian' has more pink in the bloom. *V. davidii* AGM is a low-growing evergreen with large, oval, glossy dark green leaves with characteristic linear grooves. The deciduous *V.* x *bodnantense* produces clusters of sweet-smelling pink flowers on its bare branches

ABOVE *Syringa meyeri* 'Palibin' AGM

ABOVE *Viburnum tinus* 'Gwenllian'

throughout winter, starting often as early as mid-autumn; 'Dawn' is my favourite of the cultivars available – its rose-pink blooms slowly darkening as they age. Long-lasting berries of bright blue, on reddish stalks, follow the small early summer flowers. The Guelder rose (*V. opulus*) produces amazing white ball flowers in late spring and early summer, and to my mind the finest form is 'Roseum' AGM (which is sometimes still seen under its old name of 'Sterile'). The so-called 'hobble bush' (*V. lantanoides*) is an exception in that it needs an acid soil.

NAME: *WISTERIA*

Origin: China, Japan, eastern US
Type: Twining, woody, deciduous climbers
USDA Zone: Z4–8
Preferred pH range: 6.0–8.0
Description: The showy, fragrant spring blooms are stunning. But the plants can be so vigorous

that they often burst forth in full flower before their leaves have opened. Belonging to the pea family, these climbers produce long trusses of flowers in shades of blue, purple and white. Masses of leaves are produced by mid-summer, and these turn to golden yellow in autumn, often giving wisterias a second season of interest.

Popular species and varieties: The Japanese wisteria (*Wisteria floribunda*) has fragrant pea-like blooms of blue to violet, pink or white. It is relatively manageable, with stems growing to a mere 28ft (9m) or so in length. There is a lovely white form, 'Alba', and 'Royal Purple' has double, deep purple flowers. The Chinese wisteria (*W. sinensis* AGM) on the other hand makes a huge plant extending to 100ft (30m) if allowed. It has very fragrant flowers of pale purple. Even better as a plant, although not purple, is the white form 'Alba' AGM.

BELOW *Wisteria sinensis* AGM

143

TREES, SHRUBS AND CLIMBERS, PREFERRING SOILS IN THE NEUTRAL RANGE

The following plants thrive in a soil with a pH range that straddles both the higher levels of acidity and the lower levels of alkalinity

Latin name	Common name	pH range
Carpinus	Hornbeam	6.0–7.5
Ceratostigma	Hardy plumbago	6.0–7.5
Cercis	Judas tree	6.0–7.5
Chimonanthus	Winter sweet	6.5–7.5
Cotoneaster	–	6.5–7.5
Davidia	Pocket handkerchief tree/Dove tree	6.5–7.5
Enkianthus	–	5.0–7.5
Forsythia	Golden bells	6.0–8.0
Fothergilla	–	5.0–7.5
Fraxinus	Ash	6.0–8.0
Globularia	–	5.5–7.5
Jasminum	Jasmine	6.0–7.5
Juglans	Walnut	6.5–7.5
Kerria	Jew's mallow	6.0–7.5
Leucothoe	–	6.0–7.5
Liquidambar	Sweet gum	6.0–7.5
Mahonia	Oregon grape	6.0–7.5
Photinia	–	6.0–8.0
Populus	Poplar	6.0–8.0
Pyracantha	Firethorn	6.0–8.0

ABOVE *Forsythia x intermedia* 'Spectabilis'

ABOVE *Photinia x fraseri* 'Birmingham'

VEGETABLES, FRUITS AND HERBS

Earlier in this book I alluded to the fact that there are many types of fruits and vegetables that grow well on, or even prefer, an alkaline soil. But if your soil is acid, you can still grow these alkaline-loving food crops in large tubs and containers with imported alkaline topsoil.

On the next few pages we offer a brief look at the types most suited to alkaline conditions. For more information on growing fruits and vegetables it is best to consult a more detailed book on the subject (such as *Success with Organic Fruit* and/or *Success with Organic Vegetables*, companion volumes to this book, also published by Guild of Master Craftsman Publications).

Note that in this section we lead with the common name of the fruit, vegetable or herb, followed by the botanical Latin name in brackets. This is because all gardeners refer to these plants by their common names and would be both clumsy and unnecessary to list them in a less appealing way.

NAME: BLACKCURRANT (*RIBES NIGRUM*)

Preferred pH range: 7.0–8.0

Description: Pies and puddings, yes. Jams and jellies, definitely. But would you eat blackcurrants raw? I don't think so. The word 'tart' does little to describe these little black marbles... but they're certainly worth growing as they give a good return on your investment, and they are crammed with vitamins. The currants are ripe and ready for picking about seven days after they have turned blue-black, in mid-summer. The early varieties, such as 'Boskoop Giant' and 'Laxton's Giant', should be picked promptly as the berries soon 'go over' if left on the plant.

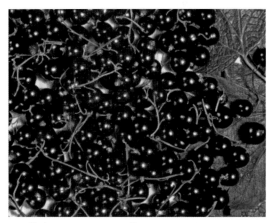

ABOVE **Blackcurrants are not usually eaten raw.**

NAME: ELDER (*SAMBUCUS NIGRA*)

Preferred pH range: 7.0–8.0

Description: A deciduous shrub or small tree, the elder is a common sight in old-style hedgerows, where its cream-white flowers in late spring are picked to make elderflower water (reputed to be good for the complexion) and the highly palatable and fragrant elderflower 'champagne'. And in the autumn its berries, rich in vitamin C, are picked for making jams, cordials and wine. This is not particularly a food subject to plant, grow and nurture, so much as a wild plant whose attributes we use. Only the species is grown in this way.

ABOVE **Elderberries are rich in vitamin C.**

ABOVE **Garlic is easy to grow.**

NAME: GARLIC (*ALLIUM SATIVUM*)

Preferred pH range: 7.0–8.0

Description: We are only just beginning to understand all of the health-giving properties of garlic. And it can be grown easily, from shop-bought bulbs. Planting should take place in early to mid-spring. Choose a sunny corner of the garden to grow them, or a large pot in a sunny spot on the patio or balcony. Dig the soil – or use fresh multi-purpose potting compost – and sprinkle a handful of organic general fertilizer, such as seaweed or blood, fish and bone. Take a bulb and split it into its clove sections, planting each section so that it is just under the surface of the soil, about 6in (15cm) apart. Only the main species is generally available.

ABOVE **Globe artichoke head.**

NAME: GLOBE ARTICHOKE (*CYNARA SCOLYMUS*)

Preferred pH range: 6.5–8.0

Description: The globe artichoke is a handsome thistle-like plant, and is frequently grown more in a flower border than a kitchen garden. It grows to about 4ft (1.2m) in height, its arching silvery leaves being most attractive. It is simple to grow, but requires a lot of space for a small yield. The allotment is the best place for it. It's a three-year crop, and plants should be discarded after the third year. From mid-summer onwards you can cut the heads off as they become available. On no account leave any on the plants so long that the scales open out, revealing a purple tinge at the base; this is the plant beginning to flower, so rendering the heads inedible. 'Green Globe' and 'Vert de Lyon' are recommended for their large, green heads.

NAME: GRAPES (*VITIS VINIFERA*)

Preferred pH range: 7.0–8.0

Description: Growing vines is a fussy business. Some varieties need lots of heat, others lots of sunshine, most like their roots cool, and they all have particular pruning, feeding and pest and disease control requirements. But the main reason why gardeners are put off them is the space they require. One plant usually needs 10ft (3m) of run, whether growing inside a greenhouse, or outdoors on a sunny wall.

'Buckland Sweetwater' is a good white grape. 'Black Hamburgh' is an early dessert variety that was at one time the most widely grown grape in Britain. The world-famous vine planted at Hampton Court Palace in England in the 1700s, which is still going strong (and which my father used to look after, but that's another story) is of this variety.

ABOVE **White grape 'Buckland Sweetwater'**

ABOVE **Olives were once considered exotic.**

NAME: LEEK (*ALLIUM PORRUM*)

Preferred pH range: 7.0–8.0

Description: This is one of the hardiest of winter vegetables – no matter how severe the frosts they will survive unharmed. From seed sown in early to mid-spring, or young plants bought and planted out in late spring or early summer, leeks come to maturity throughout the autumn and winter. The good thing about leeks is that there is no rush – they can be left in the ground until they are needed for the kitchen. They don't spoil, at least not until the weather starts to get warm again. Look for the varieties 'Hannibal' (an early autumn variety with dark green leaves and a long, thick white shank) and 'Atlanta' (with similar attributes, yet is even hardier).

NAME: OLIVE (*OLEA EUROPAEA*)

Preferred pH range: 7.0–8.5

Description: Anyone who has visited a country bordering the Mediterranean will have seen olive trees, some of them pretty ancient, laden with health-giving fruits. On a patch of wild ground these slow-growing evergreen trees can reach up to 40ft (12m) – and really old specimens can be very attractive, with their gnarled trunks and silvery leaves.

These trees can be kept in pots, on a patio or balcony, which will keep them stunted for a few years. Eventually they will need planting out, however.

Usually only the straight species is available. Search hard and you may find the sub-tropical variety 'Oblonga' for sale, or the green pickling variety 'Queen Manzanilla'.

ABOVE **Leek 'Hannibal'**

147

ABOVE **Common oregano** (*Origanum vulgare*)

NAME: OREGANO/MARJORAM (*ORIGANUM spp*)

Preferred pH range: 7.0–8.0

Description: Often called marjoram, this has a variety of flavouring uses – in salads, stuffings, with cooked meat (chicken especially), fish, egg and cheese; it's worth experimenting with. Common oregano (*Origanum vulgare*) is a slightly sprawling plant with dark green peppery-flavoured leaves. There are variegated and golden-leaved forms. Sweet marjoram (*O. majorana*) is a tender form that needs winter protection. The pot or French marjoram (*O. onites*) has mid-green savoury-flavoured leaves and white or pink flowers.

ABOVE **Pea 'Kelvedon Wonder'**

NAME: PEA (*PISUM SATIVUM*)

Preferred pH range: 7.0–8.0

Description: The most popular variety is 'Kelvedon Wonder', a sweet and heavy cropper, but there are plenty of others to try. When picked straight from the pod these are so sweet that they can be eaten raw as a snack. They are often described as round or wrinkled – not a precise description of the shape of the pea, but more as a way of classifying them as hardy (round for autumn sowing) or tender (wrinkled for spring sowing). Sow them straight outdoors in autumn or spring, 1–2in (2.5–5cm) deep and 2–3in (5–7cm) apart. Harvest them around 12 weeks after sowing.

NAME: STRAWBERRY (*FRAGARIA x ANANASSA*)

Preferred pH range: 7.0–8.0

Description: Traditionally grown in beds and borders, all types are just as successful in pots and even hanging baskets, where their tantalizing fruits hang over the sides, well away from ravenous slugs.

With early, mid-summer, late, perpetual and alpine strawberries, you could enjoy fresh strawberries for almost five months of the year. There are dozens of varieties to choose from, and you'll find different varieties for sale at the garden centre depending on when you visit. The old variety 'Cambridge Favourite' is still very popular today, because it is heavy cropping, tolerates a range of soil and keeps its fruit quality even when berries are left on the plant for a long time. Even older is 'Royal Sovereign', which produces moderate crops of large fruit in early summer and is packed full of flavour. 'Aromel' is a good modern cropper.

ABOVE Strawberry 'Aromel'

NAME: SWISS CHARD (*BETA VULGARIS* CICLA GROUP)

Preferred pH range: 7.0–8.0

Description: This is better than spinach (it's meatier), and it provides a tangier taste, too. It is quite a big vegetable, when compared to carrots and spring onions, but regardless of that it can be grown in a container. The stems are incredibly attractive. Looking akin to rhubarb, but with smaller leaves, the stalks can be in bright yellows, oranges, scarlet, almost purple or bright white. Every bit of the above-ground part of the plant is edible.

One long row of it fed my family of four for two months… so it's economical (and the price of the seeds is relatively low too: it's a win-win-win crop). Look for the cultivars 'Lucullus' (yellow-green leaves and yellow-white stalks) and 'Fordhook Giant' (broad, ivory-white stalks).

ABOVE Swiss chard comes in many bright colours.

VEGETABLES AND FRUITS PREFERRING SOILS IN THE NEUTRAL RANGE

The following plants thrive in a soil with a pH range that straddles both the lower levels of alkalinity and the higher levels of acidity

VEGETABLES

Name	pH range
Broccoli	6.0–7.5
Celery	6.0–7.5
Courgettes	5.5–7.5
Lettuce	6.0–7.5
Onion	6.0–7.5
Pepper	5.5–7.5
Radish	6.0–7.5
Rhubarb	5.5–7.5
Shallot	5.5–7.5
Swede	5.5–7.5
Turnip	5.5–7.5

FRUITS

Name	pH range
Apricot	6.0–7.5
Grape	6.0–7.5
Hazelnut	6.0–7.5
Lemon	6.0–7.5
Red currant	5.5–7.5

HERBS

Name	pH range
Chives	6.0–7.5
Horseradish	6.0–7.5
Sage	6.0–7.5
Thyme	5.5–7.5

HOUSE AND CONSERVATORY PLANTS

The pH level of soils is important to all soil-growing plants (for some plants are epiphytic – having no or few roots, and so grow on tree branches in Nature). Most house plants, it has to be said, prefer more or less acid conditions, and will therefore suffer if potted in an alkaline potting mixture. However, there are still a few of our more popular indoor plants needing higher levels of alkalinity in order to thrive, and over the next few pages we take a quick look at some of them.

For more detail on growing house plants it is best to consult a specialist book on the subject.

NAME: *ADIANTUM RADDIANUM* AGM (MAIDENHAIR FERN)

Preferred pH range: 6.5–8.0

Description: This fern produces lovely apple-green foliage that contrasts well with its black stems. Bright, direct sunlight and a dry room atmosphere will prove fatal. Stand these plants on a tray of damp pebbles, place them in light shade and in a warm room, and they will repay you with elegant growth. Feed plants in spring and summer only.

ABOVE *Asparagus meyeri*

NAME: *ASPARAGUS* spp (ASPARAGUS FERN)

Preferred pH range: 6.5–8.0

Description: *Asparagus meyeri* and *A. sprengeri* are the two most frequently seen forms. In the former, the foliage comes as pale green cylindrical plumes on stiff stems up to 2ft (60cm) long. With *A. sprengeri*, however, the foliage is wispier and arguably more fern-like. Do not overwater or overfeed these plants, as they will quickly protest by turning yellow.

NAME: *CALADIUM* spp (ANGEL-WINGS)

Preferred pH range: 6.5–7.5

Description: There are many varieties (although not usually sold named), all with large, decorative and frequently highly colourful, heart-shaped leaves. Caladiums are not the easiest of plants to care for, but when grown well they are spectacular. Avoid bright light. Avoid low temperatures – 18–24°C (65–75°F) is ideal – and use free-draining compost that is acid-free.

ABOVE *Adiantum raddianum* AGM

ABOVE *Caladium* hybrid

ABOVE *Chlorophytum* 'Bonnie'

NAME: *CHLOROPHYTUM COMOSUM* (SPIDER PLANT)

Preferred pH range: 6.5–8.0

Description: One of the most ubiquitous of house plants, the spider plant produces clumps of soft, arching, lance-shaped leaves. During the active growing period, pale yellow stems up to 2ft (60cm) long arch upward between the leaves. These carry small six-petalled white flowers, which are succeeded by little plants appearing either singly or in groups. These can be detached and rooted as new plants. The commonest form is 'Variegatum' AGM with cream-yellow bands all along the centres of the leaves. Several other forms exist, including 'Bonnie' with attractively curled leaves

NAME: *CUPHEA* spp (FIRECRACKER PLANT)

Preferred pH range: 6.5–8.0

Description: The *Cuphea* genus includes many species, but only a few are used as house plants. They are prized for their brightly coloured flowers, which bloom nearly continuously from early spring to late autumn. They generally grow to about 2ft (60cm), and have small, leathery leaves held on many branches. *Cuphea ignea* AGM is known as the cigar flower, for the individual orange blooms are tipped by a white-purple 'mouth', resembling a miniature cigar complete with ash. *C. ignea* 'Variegata' has leaves flecked with yellow.

ABOVE *Cuphea ignea* AGM

NAME: *EUPHORBIA MILII* AGM (CROWN OF THORNS)

Preferred pH range: 6.0–8.0

Description: This is a dense plant up to 3ft (90cm) tall, carrying thick dark brown stems armed on all sides and at frequent intervals with sharp spines of varying lengths. Clusters of bright green leaves last for several months before dropping off, leaving the stems bare. Old leaves are not replaced, and new ones will appear only on new terminal growth. Flowers are tiny, but each is surrounded by bright yellow and red bracts, which look like petals.

ABOVE *Euphorbia milii* AGM

ABOVE *Freesia* hybrid

ABOVE *Hibiscus rosa-sinensis* hybrid

NAME: *FREESIA* spp

Preferred pH range: 6.5–8.5

Description: Hybrid freesias are attractive, sweet-smelling plants that will flower well in a house or conservatory. They grow from corms, which should be planted up in batches from late summer to early winter for flowering in succession through to the middle of spring. The flowers are funnel-shaped and grow on the sides of wiry stems some 12–18in (30–45cm) long. Many bright colours are available, with the 'Super Giant' hybrids being high-yielding and early flowering, and in all colours.

NAME: *HIBISCUS ROSA-SINENSIS* (ROSE OF CHINA)

Preferred pH range: 6.5–8.0

Description: A shrubby evergreen plant, bearing dark-green leaves with toothed edges, the indoor *Hibiscus* does give a flavour of the exotic. Its large, showy flowers in white and shades of red, orange, yellow and pink, open out to flared trumpets, some 4–6in (10–15cm) wide, with a prominent column of fused stamens. On well-grown plants there will be a succession of flowers from spring to late summer. 'Koeniger' is double and yellow; 'Surfrider' is yellow with a red eye; 'Rosalie' is a clear rose pink; and many other modern hybrids are available.

NAME: *MANDEVILLA* spp

Preferred pH range: 6.5–7.5

Description: These are handsome plants for a sunroom or conservatory, where they can be grown in large tubs. They produce long twining stems, so should be provided with canes or a trellis, or the shoots can be cut back after flowering to keep the plant bushy. The most easily available plant is *Mandevilla* x *amabilis* 'Alice du Pont' AGM, with glossy, deep-green leaves and large funnel-shaped pink flowers, each with a throat of darker pink. Many plants from this genus used to be known as *Dipladenia*, and may still be found under this name.

ABOVE *Mandevilla x amabilis* 'Alice du Pont' AGM

ABOVE *Pellaea rotundifolia* AGM

ABOVE *Pilea* 'Moon Valley'

NAME: *PELLAEA ROTUNDIFOLIA* AGM (BUTTON FERN)

Preferred pH range: 6.5–8.0

Description: The button fern is a native of the temperate forests of New Zealand, and it produces a mass of thin dark stems that, close-up, appear to be covered with brown scales and hairs. From these stalks arise small, arched fronds of leathery green round leaflets, which trail over the edge of the pot, making it ideal for an indoor hanging basket. Unlike most ferns, this one tolerates relatively dry conditions. Only the species is normally available.

NAME: *PILEA* spp

Preferred pH range: 6.5–8.0

Description: There are a number of excellent forms of *Pilea*, all good, small foliage plants for windowsills or even a bottle garden. *Pilea cadierei* is a popular and easy plant and is called the aluminium plant because of the silvery raised patches on the otherwise green leaves. The variety 'Minima' is a dwarf form with smaller leaves. P. 'Moon Valley' has pointed, bright green, puckered leaves with dark bronze veins. P. *involucrata* is a bushy, spreading plant, with dark-green leaves tinged reddish brown and red on the undersides.

NAME: *YUCCA ELEPHANTIPES* AGM (YUCCA PLANT)

Preferred pH range: 6.5–8.0

Description: Yuccas are good architectural plants, and this is by far the most common of the house plant forms. It is usually available as a stout, woody trunk with one or two rosettes of long, sword-shaped, pointed leaves at the top. The edges of these leaves are toothed, but the leaves themselves are much softer than most other types – particularly the spiky *Yucca aloifolia* that is dangerously vicious (it is also known as the Spanish bayonet plant). There are several variegated varieties, including 'Silver Star', 'Jewel' and 'Variegata', but they are difficult to find.

ABOVE *Yucca elephantipes* AGM

HOUSE AND GREENHOUSE PLANTS PREFERRING SOILS IN THE NEUTRAL RANGE

The following plants thrive in a soil with a pH range that straddles both the higher levels of acidity and the lower levels of alkalinity

Latin name	Common name	pH range
Aglaonema	Painted drop tongue	5.0–7.5
Aphelandra	Zebra plant	5.0–7.5
Aspidistra	Cast-iron plant	4.0–7.5
Begonia	–	5.5–7.5
Calathea	Peacock plant	5.0–7.5
Calceolaria	Slipper flower	6.0–7.5
Capsicum	Ornamental pepper	5.0–7.5
Cissus	Kangaroo vine	5.0–7.5
Clivia	Kaffir lily	5.5–7.5
Crassula	Money plant/Jade plant	5.0–7.5
Fittonia	Silver net leaf	5.5–7.5
Gardenia	–	5.0–7.5
Gynura	Purple passion vine	5.5–7.5
Helxine	Mind-your-own-business	5.0–7.5
Hoya	Wax flower	5.0–7.5
Iresine	Blood leaf	5.5–7.5
Lantana	Yellow sage	5.5–7.5
Maranta	Prayer plant	5.0–7.5
Monstera	Swiss cheese plant	5.0–7.5
Phyllitis	Hart's tongue fern	6.0–8.0
Sempervivum	Houseleek	6.0–8.0

ABOVE **The Kaffir lily (*Clivia miniata*)**

ABOVE **The highly fragrant *Gardenia***

154

Glossary

Acid
With a pH value below 7; acid soil is deficient in lime and basic minerals.

Alkaline
With a pH value above 7.

Annual
Plant grown from seed that germinates, flowers, sets seed and dies in one growing year.

Bare-root
Plants sold with their roots bare of soil (i.e. not in a pot or container).

Biennial
A plant that grows from seed and completes its life cycle within two years.

Calcicole
Alkaline-loving plant; one that does not tolerate acid conditions.

Calcifuge
Acid-loving plant such as camellia, rhododendron and heather.

Cultivar
A cultivated plant clearly distinguished by one or more characteristics and which retains these characteristics when propagated; a contraction of 'cultivated variety', and often abbreviated to 'cv.' in plant naming.

Deciduous
Plant that loses its leaves at the end of every growing year, and which renews them at the start of the next.

Double
Referred to in flower terms as a bloom with several layers of petals; usually there would be a minimum of 20 petals. 'Very double' flowers have more than 40 petals.

Genus (pl. Genera)
A category in plant naming, comprising a group of related species.

Heeling in
Laying plants in the soil, with the roots covered, as a temporary measure until full planting can take place.

Humus
Organic matter that has been broken down by bacteria in the soil, resulting in a black, crumbly and fibrous substance from which plants can easily extract nutrients.

Hybrid
The offspring of genetically different parents, usually produced in cultivation, but occasionally arising in the wild.

Lime
Compounds of calcium. This can be used to 'sweeten' an acidic soil, to make it suitable for growing a wider range of plants.

Mulch
Layer of material applied to the soil surface, to conserve moisture, improve its structure, protect roots from frost and suppress weeds.

Peat

Partially decayed organic matter. Usually acid, it is used for adding to composts and mulches. For environmental reasons, it is better to use peat substitutes such as coconut fibre or bark.

Perennial

Plant that lives for at least three seasons.

Photosynthesis

The process of food manufacture in plants, whereby chlorophyll in leaves traps the sun's energy, combines it with carbon dioxide in the air and hydrogen in water and creates carbohydrates.

pH scale

A scale measured from 1–14 that indicates the alkalinity or acidity of soil. pH 7 is neutral; pH 1–7 is acid, pH 7–14 is alkaline.

Ray floret

The 'petals' of the flowers of some members of the daisy family.

Rhizome

A branched underground stem that bears roots and shoots.

Rootstock

A plant used to provide the root system for a grafted plant.

Side shoot

A stem that arises from the side of a main shoot or stem.

Single

In flower terms, a single layer of petals opening out into a fairly flat shape, comprising no more than five petals.

Species

A category in plant naming, the rank below genus, containing related, individual plants.

Sport

A mutation, caused by a genetic change (accidental or intentional) which may produce shoots with different characteristics, such as flowers with a different colour.

Sub-shrub

A plant that produces some woody mature growth, but the soft growth of which will die down in winter.

Sucker

Generally a shoot that arises from below ground, emanating from a plant's roots, but also refers to any shoot on a grafted plant that originates from below the graft union.

Topsoil

The fertile, upper-most layer of soil.

Transpiration

Part of the natural process of photosynthesis whereby plants lose water through their leaves into the atmosphere. If the transpiration rate exceeds the rate of water intake via the roots, the plant will dehydrate and start to wilt.

Variety

A naturally occurring variant of a wild species; usually shorted to 'var.' in plant naming.

About the author

Graham Clarke lives with his wife and two daughters in Dorset, on England's south coast.

Here the air is clear, with a mild climate that is far drier than most other parts of the UK.

Graham was born into gardening – literally. His father was in charge of the world-famous Regent's Park in London and at the time of Graham's birth the family lived in a lodge within the gardens there. During his formative years Graham was surrounded by quality horticulture, so it was little surprise when he chose this as his career.

He went to study with England's Royal Horticultural Society at Wisley Gardens, and after that worked as a gardener at Buckingham Palace in London. This very private garden is seen by Her Majesty the Queen on most of the days she is in residence.

For more than 25 years Graham has been a gardening writer and journalist. He has written a dozen books, and countless articles for most of the major UK gardening magazines. At various times he was editor of *Amateur Gardening* (the UK's leading weekly magazine for amateurs) and *Horticulture Week* (the UK's leading weekly magazine for professionals).

Over the years he has gardened on a wide range of soils, and his current alkaline soil (pH7.6) enables him to grow some of his favourite plants – both decorative and productive.

Index

Pages highlighted in **bold** indicate photographs of plants

GMC Publications, 166 High Street, Lewes, East Sussex BN7 1XU, United Kingdom
Tel: 01273 488005 Fax: 01273 402866
www.gmcbooks.com

Contact us for a complete catalogue, or visit our website